Proper Balance Movement:
A Diary of Lameness

Tony Gonzales·

REF Publishing
Manassas ● Virginia

REF Publishing
REF Typesetting & Publishing, Manassas, Virginia

Text © 1986, 1988, 1991 A.Z. Gonzles

First Edition Published in 1986
Third Edition Published in 1991
Printed in the United States of America

91   92   93   94   6   5   4   3

Library of Congress Cataloging in Publication
Card Number: 86-060039

ISBN 0-9612862-6-1

Available from
Anthony Z. Gonzales
13602 Ellendale Dr.
Chantilly, VA 22021

Cover Photo by
David E. James
Box 172, RD #3
Lewistown, PA 17044

REF Publishing
9400 Fairview Ave.
Manassas, VA 22110
(703) 631-1115

Text set in Camelot with sidebars in Windsor Elongated at the
REF Typesetting & Publishing Center, Manassas, VA 22110

Dedication

**From the Hand of God
into the Hands of Mankind
a Horse was Delivered.**

—Zac

I would like to dedicate this book to several people who had patience with me over the years. First to my father, for without his guidance and wisdom I would not have been able to accomplish this dream. To my wife Robyn for her patience and encouragement to go for my dream. To my daughters Carrie and Sherry who were patient with me during my long hours at the typewriter. To my brother Moses who helped me discover P.B.M. and gave it its name. To my brothers Matthew, Abraham and Billy for allowing me to teach them and to my Mother for putting up with me during my younger years. To Mike Mascaroni for teaching me common sense. To Sonny Boy, my horse for 21 years, for giving me insight that horses are people too. To Drs. Rooney and Callahan for giving me insight into veterinary medicine and to Pat for dreams of rocking chairs. To Edwin Elliott and the staff of REF for helping me accomplish my dream. To my clients who have been patient and faithful, and most of all to the almighty God for showing me the way.

Lord,

make me an instrument of thy peace
WHERE there is hatred—let me sow love
WHERE there is injury—pardon
WHERE there is doubt—faith
WHERE there is despair—hope
WHERE there is darkness—light
and WHERE there is sadness—joy.

Prayer of St. Francis of Assisi

Table of Contents

Dedication iii
A Horseman's Prayer iv
Introduction vii
Chapter 1 — Curvature of the Spine 1
    Cindy's Story
Chapter 2 — Balance the Hoof 17
    Definitions
Chapter 3 — Abcessed Foot 27
    King's Story
Chapter 4 — Ringbone 39
    Small Fry's Story
Chapter 5 — Navicular 47
    Jim's Story
Chapter 6 — Balance the Horse 61
    Definitions
Chapter 7 — Movement Problem 69
    Debby's Story
Chapter 8 — Arthritic Knee 83
    Bojangles' Story
Chapter 9 — Conformation Fault 99
    Beau's Story
Chapter 10 — Splay Footed 107
    Topper's Story
Chapter 11 — Balance the Rider 119
    Definitions
Chapter 12 — Shoulder Problem 133
    Justice's Story
Chapter 13 — Ringbone and Spavin 153
    Miss Clooney's Story
Chapter 14 — Attitude Problem 163
    Moses' Story

Chapter 15 — Splints 175
            Fancy's Story
Chapter 16 — Vertebrae Problem 187
            Marsha's Story
Chapter 17 — Philosophy 195
            Definition
Charts 203
Explanation of Charts 208
Bibliography 211

Introduction

Publishing is an addictive business. It gets inside and changes the way people think. After a time a publisher starts getting a kick out of anything that goes on paper. Some editors get to the point that they check the copy on cereal boxes at breakfast.

Then somebody walks into the office with a totally new idea and everything breaks loose. The coffee cups get shoved back and the pencils come down off the ears and a hush settles in thick as a spring fog on the Blue Ridge.

It doesn't happen often, but when it does nothing can match the high.

When Tony Gonzales walked into my office followed by a couple of apprentices decked out in field gear I frankly wasn't expecting to see a manuscript that would change millions of lives. Five minutes later I was a convert mentally calculating how long this one could stay on the market. Publishers go to sleep dreaming about the big one that stays on the list for years.

The big books always involve discovering the obvious. And that is just what Tony has done. He put it this way,

I had to question everything. That is

always the first rule for a radical. I wasn't trying to prove the theory wrong, but I needed to fully understand why we put on these shoes. While making these investigations, I started looking for another way.

Seeing and understanding what you see are two different processes. Ask any old horse-shoer and he will tell you about farriers he knew when he was starting who could scan a horse and tell all kinds of things about the animal. Perhaps he couldn't put his knowledge into words, but he understood more than what falls below the knee.

Tony is in touch with this older holistic approach, but he adds to it the aggressive drive of a good investigative reporter. The product is a book which will be the first textbook in an entire new science of horseshoeing.

By adding together judgment, discernment, and compassion, Tony came up with Proper Balance Movement. Admittedly, horses are only perfect as they are found in each owner's mind and heart, but even radically defective animals can be made sound and safe with the right attention.

That attention will make a multi-million dollar change in the American horse business. Lameness will never go away, but it can be treated, corrected, and often it actually can be prevented.

P.B.M. is also going to make a difference in the relationship of the several horse professions. Farriers trained in Tony's system are actually equine kinesiologists who correspond to the nurse practioners or physician's assistants who began appearing in human medicine over the last two decades. The farriers are not going to practice medicine, but as they make the records they need for their new science, they will be compiling information about horses which will be worth its weight in gold to the veterinarian when he treats the horses. Riding instructors are going to need this information too. In time, the three disciplines, which have not always worked well together, are going to grow obviously dependent on each other.

It is difficult to break new ground when the professionals already have an answer for everything. Tony had the good judgment to take this into consideration and to develop his theory slowly, testing each concept in real life and discussing each element with key thinkers in the field before going public. Frankly it shows. Scientists and very ordinary horselovers both from all over the world have been proving this theory for five years.

The time for this book has arrived and I couldn't be prouder to be the publisher.

Edwin P. Elliott, Jr.
REF Publishing
March 15, 1986
Manassas, Virginia

Chapter 1

Cindy's Story

"She's what? Mentally retarded!"

It was a typical Thursday evening in the life of a busy horseshoer—home after a hard day's work, only to spend another hour trying to contact customers. Several potential customers had left messages the night before and during the day.

Looking over the stack of notes, one jumped out at me—a distress call from a man named Jeff. He was not a regular customer, but I remembered a Jeff from grade school. My

Baffled Professionals

fingers dialed the number, and a mildly familiar voice filled my ear. It was the same Jeff, after all these years. He also remembered me, so we shot the breeze about old times.

Then the subject turned to business. Jeff had bought a young Percheron filly named Cindy about a year and a half earlier. At that time he didn't know that he was buying potentially serious trouble.

Tragedy began unfolding for my old friend. Cindy was a beautiful little horse but she wouldn't do anything right. If you look far enough every horse can do something—but not Cindy.

The professionals were baffled.

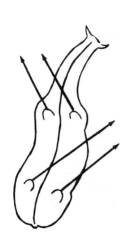

On the phone Jeff called it a no win situation. The filly had gotten three different diagnoses and each had the same outcome—no cure.

The first diagnosis was the most logical. The filly had the wobbler syndrome. Since I had never before heard of this condition, Jeff introduced me to the subject. He had been told that the wobbler syndrome arose from possible degeneration of vertebrae in the animal's hind end. The process causes the horse to lose motor control of the hind end.

However, it was going to take more than a strange new name for her problem to help Cindy.

The next diagnosis claimed the filly suffered from having a pinched nerve in the neck.

A Mentally Retarded Horse!

The final, and wildest, diagnosis was mental retardation. Pausing a moment for quick thought, I suddenly started to question the sanity of my profession. A mentally retarded horse! Still Jeff had received good professional diagnoses—there had been a lot of thought and observation involved in each diagnosis of the filly.

Now it was my turn and my old friend was asking me for something more than, "Put her down. There is no hope."

Jeff explained that he came to me when he heard I was experimenting on a new system of shoeing that seemed to work miracles. He was looking for a reason to hope that his filly could be healed. Obviously Jeff loved this animal. He had no intention of having her put to sleep.

It was important to warn him that I did not have all the answers, the work was still in the experimental stage. Even so I could hold out hope to him and I was determined to try.

There are very few books on horse anatomy and horse professionals often refuse to share knowledge. No one was going to help me and I did not know much about the filly. At the same time I had always found answers for every problem.

New Cause, New Discoveries, New Answer

Arrangements were made to meet Jeff on Saturday afternoon at two o'clock. I kept the rest of the afternoon available to allow adequate time for working on the filly without worrying about other distractions. It was difficult enough to cope with the problems I had given myself.

You see, I had done what horseshoers have done for years, putting myself out on a limb for a horse and its owner. Suddenly the usual emotions began to hit: fear, apprehension, excitement, and curiosity.

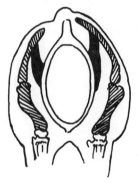

The fear sprang from the possibility of failure. How much could I learn about the horse's problem? Would I cause the filly further harm?

Apprehension came from not wanting to offend anyone if I should find another cause for the problem. I knew at the time I had already set myself up for public criticism.

Excitement came from the process of logical thinking that had now taken control of my mind. A problem means a new cause, a chance of new discoveries, and, possibly, a new answer for future reference.

Curiosity came from never having seen a mentally retarded horse.

Saturday found me anxious to start on Jeff's horse. I could hardly wait for the clock to move its hands to two o'clock. One of my younger brothers, Abraham, came to help me in case I needed some help handling the horse. I didn't know if this young filly was going to allow me to do anything to her hooves without rebelling.

Face-to-Face With Jeff

As I traveled down the dirt driveway, I could not help being deeply jealous of the person who lived on this little ranchette. The vegetation around the farm consisted of a well planned landscape of flowers and trees planted by someone who had a definite idea of what the future character and employment of this place was going to be. The view was breathtaking, with mountains in the background and the ocean in the front. Driving past the main house, there was a smaller house, probably where one of the workers lived. Across from the house was a small barn consisting of two stalls. In front of the barn there were strange vehicles the likes of which I had never seen before, a special kind of horse trolley.

When I pulled up, I expected someone to emerge from the worker's house. Instead, I heard a voice coming from one of the stalls. It was Jeff. Appearing from the stall was a man about my height, 5 feet 7 inches, with a thin coating of red curly hair on his head. He was dressed casually for sloppy barn work. We greeted each other as if it had not been 16 years since we last met.

Jeff was ready to reveal more of the story to me face to face. When Jeff bought the filly, it was not long after her weaning that he noticed

the filly did not run around. This was definitely not common behavior for a baby. He said at first he thought that this was normal behavior, that the baby was just depressed. Then she seemed to grow worse.

As the filly grew older, the filly developed an obvious movement problem. She was having a hard time walking out to the pasture. She moved slowly and became stubborn about leaving her stall. Many times Jeff would actually find the filly standing right up against the fence.

My anxiety now grew into impatience. I wanted to see this unusual filly.

Jeff showed an obvious emotional attachment to his horse, much as if the filly was part of the family. My friend was a smart man, the owner of his own company and financially well off. And he had made this horse a major part of his life and his family's life. Perhaps he had not acted out of logic, but he had found a reason to believe in this horse. Cindy could be a means of joy and instruction to him, his wife, and his children. I sent Abraham to get the filly from her stall while I assured Jeff that I would do everything humanly possible for the filly. Actually, I was really trying to reassure myself that there was some chance of helping him.

Here I found myself facing what was probably the biggest challenge of my life. As a horseshoer, I had exhausted every conceivable shoeing technique that I knew based on the information I had received on Thursday. As a horseowner I could identify with Jeff's situation, both his emotional attachment and the family's attachment as well. Also, there was more than cold logic involved. I guess I really believe in miracles.

Leftward Ho!

Don't misunderstand. This was not a claim that I, personally, was someone special. The filly was really the special one. As Abraham pulled the filly out of the stall, she showed signs of reluctance. She hugged the right side of the doorway and, as she approached I began to understood why. Cindy ended up walking on Abraham.

The filly was steadily moving to the left. Perhaps you have seen a little dog walk down a street sideways as if his tail were racing with its head.

When she stepped on Abraham, his reaction was the same as the others before him. He turned to hit the filly. Pain tends to do a man's thinking for him.

An Abused Filly

In her defense against Abraham she threw up her head and, even more vigorously, pushed him out of her way. Jeff had explained that the filly was being beaten by her handlers, basically because they were unaware of the filly's problems. When I finally got the filly to stand quietly, without any fear of reprisal, I started my observation of her physical characteristics.

**Front End
Movement Left**

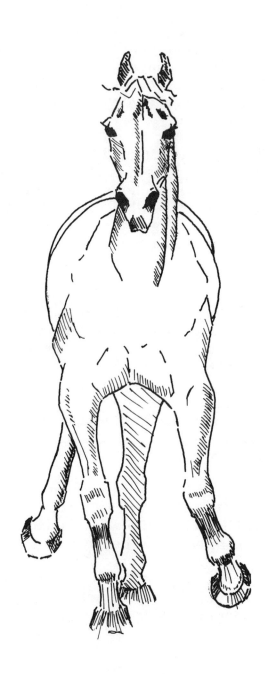

**Hind End
Movement Right**

It is often helpful when you analyze a horse to start with its eyes first. The eye shows more of the horse's present state of mind and offers an introduction to its true personality. All horses start with kind eyes, but distress, confusion, and pain can distort its appearance and size.

Kind-Eyed But Distressed

The filly's eye was full of confusion. Apparently the confusion was caused by the filly's inability to understand her physical problem and from uncertainty over what humans were expecting of her.

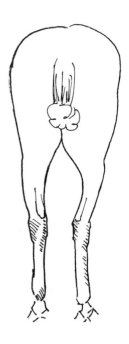

As I examined her body, starting with the front legs, an important part of her problem became obvious. This filly was my first really uneven horse. The front left leg was as much as two inches longer than the right front leg. Standing on top of one of the trolleys to get a shoulder view, I found the left shoulder was high and more developed than the right. Even more startling were the hips. From this view the right hip was at least an inch and a half higher than the left. To confirm that estimate of the length difference, I started to build up the right front leg, using groups of hoof pads to attain an even height. I asked both Jeff and Abraham to check the before and after changes to see if they also saw what I was seeing. They reached the same conclusion.

An Uneven Filly

Unbalanced, Cindy's front feet drifted left and her hind feet pulled to the right. The imbalance was turning the normal movement pattern

Lifting Pads

against itself and confusing the horse. With pads to raise the two short feet level with the two long feet the filly would be balanced. Clearly, adding two inches of padding in the front and an inch and a half in the back would be radical.

One other thing was important. I had to take into consideration the underdeveloped muscles as well as the overdeveloped muscles. To succeed, the treatment would have to promote the growth of muscle while avoiding tearing by promoting the relaxation of overdeveloped muscle.

To test my hypothesis, I directed Abraham to walk the filly before and after I balanced her.

Then I added pads to the back legs. This filly was a real sweetheart, evidently she was able to sense that we were trying to help her.

A Shock Absorbed

I chose to use pads instead of cutting one of the longer feet. When the hoof is lifted by the pads the shock is absorbed as the hoof strikes the ground. A solid substance hitting the ground would send stronger shock waves to the bones and muscles of the leg. I compromised by adding an inch and a half on the right front and an inch on the left hind.

Cindy showed no sign of resistance when I put on her first set of shoes. Again, it was as if she knew we were trying to help. I saw a spark of hope in Jeff's eyes. It also showed in the sound of

**Observant
Abraham**

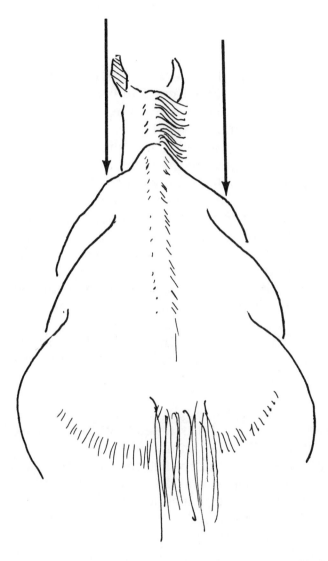

his voice. Abraham, who had been quiet all this
time, just observing, began contributing to our
hope-filled conversation. When the last hoof was
shod and the job completed, you could have cut

the air around us with a knife, it was so thick with anticipation.

Hooray! Straight Line Movement!

As excited as we were, no one wanted to make the first move. Even Cindy was apprehensive. Finally, I asked Abraham to lead the filly on a walk down the road. To our amazement, the filly no longer walked to the left. No longer did her rear end move to the right. She was moving straight. I had Abraham walk the filly for us for a while, not trusting what we were seeing. I then took the filly myself and walked her to prove that I was not influencing Jeff's vision. Abraham saw the same thing. I then gave Abraham back the filly to see if she would trot. When she did, it really took me by surprise. As I turned to Jeff, to share my jubilation, he turned away from me. As his voice cracked, he asked, "Do you realize this is the first time in about a year and a half . . . this is the first time I've seen her trot." He had tears in his eyes.

Beginning Awareness Of Curvature

Abraham brought the filly back to us and gave her to Jeff. Jeff started to walk her back to the stall. I told Abraham to get into the truck and I told Jeff we would settle the bill later. As we drove away in jubilation at what we had seen and done, I suddenly realized that horses have a long leg in their body structure, and they can also have a short leg.

This case also was the beginning of my awareness that horses can have curvature in their bodies. Later it became obvious that this curvature originates in the spine. Cindy also

12

showed me how effective an intelligent and practical shoeing technique can be in relieving major distress for the horse, improving its temper, reducing its confusion, and freeing the movement of the horse to where its muscles can lose their uneven development and acquire a normal conformation.

Relief Of Pain, Development Of Muscles

Jeff took a "mentally retarded" horse and made her into a family horse, used to pack around the children. Relieving the filly's pain, and redeveloping her muscles, enabled her to take her rightful place within the family.

The marvelous success with Cindy taught me to look for a connection between movement and body development. Cindy's uneven development was not due to improper riding—she had never been good enough to ride! She became this way on her own without any real exercise.

In more detail, her condition was as follows. She had a wide chest. The frontal muscle development of her front legs was greater than that at the rear, toward her elbow joint. Looking at her front, from the point of her shoulder back, she slanted inward toward her body rather than even or outward. This was an obvious sign of muscle atrophy. She had not been using herself right.

In her motion of the left front leg, it became apparent that she had to throw the leg to

13

Under She Goes

the outside in order to walk and maintain balance. As the leg would swing to the outside, the muscle pull would be from the chest cavity, thus developing the broadness of her chest. This movement was more comfortable for her. She moved her shoulder in accordance to the curve in the spine, seeking to minimize pain. Exercising barefoot meant that there was no influencing factor from rider's weight. As the left front leg was going outside the line of the body, the right front was traveling inward, close to the center of the body line. The same was happening to the left hind leg. It was travelling straight forward and under the body line, the right hind was traveling outward and rotating forward. This explained the upper hip muscle development pulling method. Also, before she was shod, she would stand with the left front leg out and forward, and the right would appear severely cow hocked.

The professional diagnoses had been close to the mark. The pinched nerve diagnosis identified her intense pain. However, it was possible to relieve her.

Muscle atrophy looks like vertebrae degeneration, the other diagnosis. It also contributed to her strange walk.

In some ways all three diagnoses were very reasonable. They were simply incomplete.

From weaning, Cindy had never known a time when she could walk or trot in a normal fashion. Many owners would have put her down quickly rather than pay out feed and stable costs for no practical gain. She was fortunate to have an owner who was willing to pay and work to have her healed, who hoped against hope that she could be the family horse he believed she could be. As for me, the lesson was simple. Even complex and difficult problems can have simple causes.

Difficult Problem, Simple Cause

15

After having read Tony Gonzales'
articles in the American Farriers Journal I had
the opportunity to work with him and see
his P.B.M. technique in practice.

Believe me it really works. Tony's
knowlege of anatomy and how it relates to
the balance and movement of the horse is
outstanding.

I have used his P.B.M. technique in
my own work with very satisfactory
results.

C.E. Smith
A.F.A.—WSFA

Chapter 2

Balance The Hoof

What does balance mean to me?
Balancing the hoof?

1. Normal Balance

People often ask what balance means to me. There are three answers to this question. Balance means balancing the horse's hoof. Also, balance means balancing the natural horse's conformation. Finally, balance means balancing a horse to carry its rider's weight.

When I started horseshoeing, I was not interested in balancing anything but a horse's foot. Later, I found that there is a whole realm yet to be explored in the world of horses. I will break down each section to make my presuppositions and theories clearer.

To balance the foot, all horseshoers are taught to level the ground side of the hoof. Then

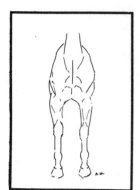
2. Frontal Width Balance

**Leveling
Was
Always
Temporary**

**Focus
On The
Hoof**

level the coronary band of the hoof in order to make the horse level in the foot. Even as I tried to perfect this technique, I only obtained minimal results. Every shoeing of the same horse would be a repeat of what had been done previously. The balance leveling was always temporary.

Often the animals would get sore to some degree. This soreness would not be noticeable right away. Instead, it usually arose after at least three shoeings. As a horseshoer, I was taught not to look above the knee, and that my concentration should focus on the hoof. At this time, very few people were talking about joint alignment.

Textbooks on horse anatomy teach that joint alignment should appear as a straight line down the center of the leg. This line would start from the middle of the knee and travel down to the middle of the hoof. The alignment is the same for the front legs and the hind legs. The basic theory to straighten a horse called for aligning the pastern bones from the side view of the leg. From this view, the line ran from the fetlock joint to the middle of the hoof. This meant that the long pastern bone, short pastern bone, and coffin bone were in straight alignment.

This information is still important. It is a significant factor in judging balance of the hoof. Proper Balance Movement simply adds a few more areas to take into consideration. For example, consider the side to side balance of the hoof. This takes into account the width of the hoof and how it affects the weight-bearing surface of the horse.

To most people, flares in the hoof are considered out of balance. Actually, they are an indication that the horse has a balance problem on that particular side. The flare develops in order to help the animal balance its weight on its hooves. This is particularly true of horses that are narrow in their bodies. The flare will be more pronounced when the animal has its legs under itself, a narrow base. Drop a plumb line or put a horseshoe nail or pen at one end of the string, then drop the line from the side of the horse's shoulder near the elbow joint of the front leg (the tricep muscle) to the side of the hoof. The flare will align with the line.

Flares are related to the narrowness of the chest cavity. A narrow chest does not allow expansion of the front legs, so when the legs are too narrow the only way the horse can maintain balance for its own body weight is for it to flare out. This becomes true for the hind legs as well. A horse that is narrow behind (cow hocked) does not have good inner thigh muscle development. Then there is nothing to support the legs, to keep them from touching at the hocks. If one were to drop a line from the hip joint down to the outside of the hoof, one would find that there would be an alignment with that flare as well. Occasionally the flare will exceed the line, but normally one would find alignment. Believe it or not, if a line could be dropped from the front of the chest down to the hoof, it would be apparent that the

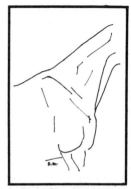

3. Right Shoulder View

Flares In The Hoof

Narrow Legs

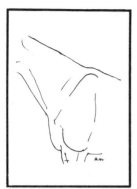

4. Left Shoulder View

toe of the hoof was reaching out to balance in front. The same goes for the hind legs, unless the horse is slightly sickle hocked.

The balance line for the hind end comes by standing behind a horse and drawing a straight line from the center of the hind leg down the center of the hock, one to the center of the fetlock and one to the center of the heels of the hoof. This means there are three lines instead of one. What can be done with all these lines?

Three Straight Lines

Start with the front legs. The three lines align the hoof with the joints in the horse's legs. These lines actually show the alignment of the horse's legs. The outside line will show what the shape of the knee is. Does the knee actually open toward the outside, or inward, or straight? The outside line can reveal the same thing for the fetlock. This line also reveals where the cannon bone is set in relation to the outside of the leg, and to the hoof. The outside line reveals where the pressure of the weight carrying surface will be. The inside lines are actually guides. The center line provides a guide to straightness. This line shows how far off to the inside or outside a horse's foot is, in proportion to the leg.

Joint Analysis

Analysis of the joints can help avoid a lot of irritation for the horse. When a horse is young and unridden, the straightness of its legs can be influenced by trimming. An older horse has its bones set, and the formation of the joints produces wear in accordance with how the movement of the horse has developed in relation to its body development. This is why horseshoers are unable to correct a horse's stance by dropping the outside or inside of the foot.

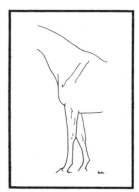

5. **Frontal Balance View**

My research has suggested some reasons for failures and successes. Most failures occur with horses that are narrow and splay footed (foot turns to the outside), or they have over-developed muscles and are pigeontoed (foot turns to the inside). For years shoeing methods were blamed for the failures, but now it is clear that failure is due to the muscle development of the front legs. Remember the front legs of a horse are connected to the trunk of the horse's body by muscle alone. Therefore, the muscle development influences whether the leg turns one way or the other. On a narrow horse, the lack of shoulder muscles and chest muscles holds the upper shoulder bones closer to the body. This forces the front legs to turn out for balance support. The pigeontoed horse has the opposite problem. Its inner shoulder and chest muscles are overdeveloped, which pushes the lower shoulder and leg bones to the outside of the body. This forces the toes to turn in for balance. Horseshoers who follow the motion of these legs, understand why the splay footed horse will grow more hoof on the outside wall. Break over shows the leg going more in than out. The toe of the hoof will always travel forward rather than back. This causes the forward paddling. Then the pigeontoed horse will grow more hoof on the inside wall. Break over would show the leg going more out than in. The toe of

Failures

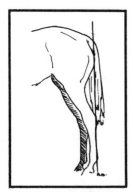

6. Hind Balance View

the hoof will be travelling more backward than forward. This causes the back paddling.

Successes

Successes occur when the upper bones rotate in accordance with the shoeing that is done. This is accomplished when the upper muscle structure absorbs any stress that the lower leg receives. This is not to say that there will not be any joint damage, but such damage would really depend on the type of work the animal was doing. Incidentally, the hind end is virtually the same as the front end. Its connection to the skeletal spine consists of muscle alone. The major difference between the hind and front ends is that the hind end involves a closer and tighter network of muscle, ligament and tendon networking. The muscle network has an influence on whether a leg will straighten up or stay the same. To straighten up most horses in their legs, there has to be some elasticity in the muscles. If the muscles lack elasticity, the animal should have an exercise program developed simultaneously with the shoeing corrections, if the corrections are not to harm the horse.

One-Stop Shoeing

The greatest problem with attempts to straighten up a horse's legs in one shoeing was the temporary nature of any solution. With this new system to test and correct how straight each horse's legs are, I have more sound straight legged horses than ever before. This does not mean I am right and everyone else is wrong. I am simply recommending a system that works.

In leveling the ground surface of the hoof, I don't like to take too much sole off the hoof. The sole adds cushion, as well as protection for the sensitive, living tissue of the inner hoof. The frog should also be carefully trimmed. When I found out that the whole sole moves to the ground, I became aware of the danger from stone bruises that exposing too much live tissue would bring.

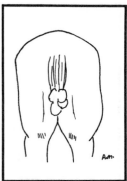

7. Hind Width Balance

In sighting the hoof, I do not put my thumb up to the heels of the foot. This would allow the thumb pressure to push one side up more than the other. Then the thumb pressure would really balance the foot for the observer. Most horseshoers do this unconsciously. Normally, they also try to level the foot to the coronary band (this is the top of the hoof where the hoof wall and hair line meet). I prefer to sight the hoof from the fetlock.

Sighting The Hoof

Hold the leg in hand at the fetlock joint. Then sight it by viewing how the lower leg comes out of the knee joint. Look at the back of the knee while holding the leg in hand. By holding the leg very loosely, one can see the alignment that one will be working toward, right on down to the hoof. This method gives me my coronary band alignment and helps the horses I shoe to walk off straight, and stay sound. This alignment can also be checked by looking at the toe wear of the shoe. One will know how a horse is breaking over by the toe wear. Signs of wear may be more confusing with a horse that paws the ground all the time.

Hold Leg In Hand

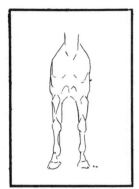

9. Splay Footed

In normal conditions, it will be apparent if a horse is moving correctly because there will be very little wear on the soles. Light wear indicates a very light mover. A horse which has a hoof with an inside hoof wall that is longer should be cut on the hoof, starting from the last nail hole which would be used in placing a shoe on the inside and cutting towards the first nail hole of the outside. This allows the heels to maintain height and allows the adjustment of the horse to be minimal but effective. Horses that interfere, hitting their ankles with the opposite hoofs, can be effectively helped using this method. It also helps decrease the swing of the leg. Further, it relieves pressure points that can push against the joints.

Decreasing The Swing

When a horse has a joint that is not aligned with the rest of the leg, this difficulty will also influence a horse's movement. There often is no correction for this. In the front leg, there should be concern for the knee joint, the fetlock joint, the short and long pastern joint and the short pastern and coffin joint.

Three Knee Joint Positions

The knee joint actually has three positions for which it can be set. The first setting is straight. This means when the knee opens, it opens straight forward, the perfect setting. The second setting is where the knee joint sets inward. This means that the knee opens inward, thus producing the outward swing of the leg, like a pigeon-toed horse. The third setting is the knee that opens outward. This is the worst knee motion. This setting produces an inward swing of the leg. I have seen swings where the horses hit the insides of their knees, their fetlock joints, and even where the horses fall down because their legs tangle up movement.

Too much correction all at once can encourage lameness problems such as knee chips, and splints. Notice I said encourage. Corrective shoeing rarely causes these problems but can increase the stress. Admittedly, this is controversial.

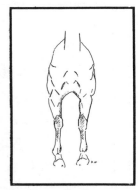

10. Pigeon Toed

Combining my knowledge of fourth level dressage riding and my 25 years of horseshoeing, I have an exciting future ahead of me. Through the teaching of P.B.M., I am now able to understand why it is important to link riding and shoeing in balancing a horse. As a horseshoer I never saw the whole horse and as a rider I never knew what the uneven movement was telling me.

Trevor Norris
Cape Town, South Africa

Chapter 3

King's Story

**"If you can't help me, then I will have
a big financial loss."**

There are days when you sometimes wish
that no one had ever heard of you—or at least
that no one would recommend you. Sometimes
people expect miracles. To them, you have
become the last resort.

Bob called one day. From the tone of his
voice, it was clear that this was another desperate call. "Hello, I'm Bob. I hear that you are the
guy that can help me."

A.M.

A Desperate Bob

Whenever someone is trying that hard to believe there is some prospect of success, you know he is hoping against hope. Bob was desperate because he was running into financial difficulties—he was on the verge of bankruptcy. He owned a Percheron stallion and 12 mares. The stallion had a bad foot. The diagnosis was pedal ostitis. This is a degeneration of the coffin bone, which causes great pain for the horse. The stallion developed an abcess in the right front foot, where the pedal ostitis is. The abcess was in the drainage hole for the infection in the hoof. Bob told me, "I hear you are working on a new theory. Perhaps you can find a way to help both me and the horse as well."

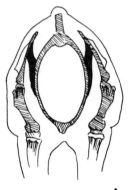

Treatment of this horse was costing Bob a lot of time and money. Beyond the cost of medications, he explained that he had to build a special stall for the stallion. The stall would keep the foot free from dirt to reduce the infection. It was hard not to be sympathetic towards his difficulties.

A Stallion With A Bad Foot

No one likes to hear that someone is nearly bankrupt, but there is always a reason for it. How did the man get into financial difficulties? Were there poor business practices, or bad advice? Perhaps he got in too deep, had too much overhead, or lost track of his expenses. It was true, he had gotten in over his head, but there was nothing wrong with his intentions.

Bob had a dream—he was going to breed horses that would make him famous. He was no different from the people who dream of raising the next Kentucky Derby winner, or the horse that goes to the Olympics. I understood Bob, because I wanted to raise the quarter horse that could win the All-American futurity in New Mexico. And I failed. My mare produced twins, and one died. The one that lived had so many leg problems, my dream was shattered. Perhaps, having failed in my dream, I had learned enough to help Bob save something worthwhile out of the shattered pieces of his dream. "I got in over my head," he said. "It's a dream gone bad."

My New Dream: Find Answers

I was in the same boat. My new dream was to find answers that would help the future of the horse world. Meanwhile, the time I was putting into my research was not being compensated monetarily. I, too, knew how much a dream can cost if it starts going bad.

I tried to be careful not to let bitterness from all the professional criticism interfere with pursuing my personal goals. When the business starts to succeed, the surrounding community starts attacking. People become afraid when they don't understand. Some experts take offense because you don't turn to them for answers. However, problems started when I asked questions of knowledgeable people and did not get worthwhile answers. Most times, I received the standard book answer.

The Standard Book Answer

I didn't let the professional critics stop me. Each attack made me work harder to develop my ideas. But I was more fortunate than Bob.

Sympathy And Curiosity

Even though I had invested a lot of time and money in my research, I didn't have mouths to feed as he had.

In this case, with both sympathy and curiosity, there was no question of refusing to help. I was not going to refuse any case just because there was a possibility of failure. There is always some insight to be learned.

I set the appointment for Saturday. This would allow some time to work on the animal. The case was going to be a first for me. I knew I had nothing to lose. After doing some book work, I realized the information was pointing me toward one answer—a bar shoe, perhaps with clips. This would give the horse even support all the way around its foot. The pressure would no longer ride in just one area. A pad might be necessary, depending on the severity of the abcess.

Why An Abcess?

The abcess kept coming up in my mind. Why an abcess? I knew that the abcess was being treated in the right manner, but something in the back of my mind refused to let it go.

When I arrived at the ranch, it was like entering another world. An eight foot high fence told me this was going to be a new world. Inside of the post were a series of straight wires, but outside, the boards that lined the perimeter were telephone poles. Yes, telephone poles. At the end of the driveway, I entered a courtyard.

A. Pettit-Massie
Jan. 1986

The gracious barn held 12 standing stalls, and in these stalls were the biggest rear ended horses I had ever seen. Bob emerged from the barn. He greeted me and took me to see the stallion. As impressive as the surroundings were, what I now saw really left me awestruck. The stallion was a mountain of a horse, the biggest animal that I had ever seen. Others had been taller but he was the broadest and the heaviest. Bob told me the horse weighed close to one ton. That means almost 2,000 pounds.

A 2,000 Pound Horse

God must love me because He gave King a great temperament. Considering what the horse

Uneven Body Pressure

was going through, he was marvelous. When we approached the stall to examine King's foot, one knew intuitively that this horse was a prisoner, not only of his leg problem, but also because he was a stallion.

The stall was large enough for the horse to move around quite a bit, but the flooring was all concrete, with no bedding. An exclusively concrete stall is puzzling. However, King needed the room and there wasn't a protective boot that would fit. Concrete would help keep the foot clean.

Bob was getting tired of his ordeal—several times a day, he had to clean the stall and then take a water hose and rinse the flooring. Fear of losing the animal to infection forced the routine on the owner. I really didn't know if I could help the stud, but there was cause for hope. It appeared that the lameness horses sometimes have is due to uneven pressure in the horse's body, creating a specific pressure point. The concrete floor in the stallion's stall helped me get a good level sighting of the horse's body and leg conformation. I was still awestruck at the size of the animal, and I remember very vividly repeating the words, "This horse is a mountain."

Sadness And Sores

It was very hard to determine if the horse was muscle bound or just plain fat. He had been doing nothing. One sad part of his imprisonment was the sight of sores that King was developing from occasionally lying down on the concrete— probably to take the strain, and pain, off his legs.

The most obvious focal point for me was the neck. King's mane seemed to fall to the horse's left side. Stallions have heavy-crested necks in many cases, in this case it was hard to tell if this was a factor. I didn't have enough experience working with horses his size to have any confidence in my judgment of his conformation.

Where Is The Mane?

The next focal point was the front legs.

This was the site that really bothered. I noticed something that I had never noticed on another horse. The front left knee had a round shape to it and the right knee had a normal shape. Examination of the hind end showed that the hips were higher than the front end. The horse's weight distribution was obviously toward the front. Then I picked up the stallion's left front leg to examine the abcess hole.

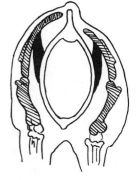

It had been opened very wide so that it would not close. Clearly I could not do anything for the abcess, After all, this really was not my department. As I put the foot down, I stood back, away from the stallion's front end looking again at his neck and front legs. Immediately Bob wanted to know what I was going to do, but I needed time to think.

Tilting To The Left

Observing the horse for perhaps the tenth time, I saw something that threw me for a loop. From the front view, here was a horse that was actually tilted to the left. His neck was leaning that way, but the rest of his body also seemed to

A Crooked Horse

be off-center. I asked Bob to help confirm my eyesight. He could find no difference, and stated that no one else saw the difference in the knees either. This did not surprise me, because we all are commonly blind towards what we see in front of us. When we look for something, it is always to be found in the most difficult spots, at least, never in the obvious place. This was a case where my quest for knowledge had given me the ability to look at the obvious for answers. This picture of a crooked standing horse gave me a whole new train of thought. I examined the animal's withers to see if I could feel the actual top of the front shoulder blades. This would help determine the height of each front leg. When I examined the withers, I estimated the height points to have as much as one and a half inches difference. The right front leg was longer.

Pressure Point Theory

This difference appeared to be a real boost to my theory on pressure points. In this case, there seemed to be a pressure point in the right front leg that was keeping the abcess irritated. It was interesting to note that the abcess was on the outside of the right front foot. Bob and I considered the reasons for this location, and he began to understand my point. Obviously the stance was having a direct effect on the horse's problem.

What can be done practically to adjust the stance? One choice was to lift the left front leg in order to help straighten the horse's body. Who could guess what that weight transferral would do to the other side? The height of the hind end had to be considered, and it was important to know how it would affect any attempt at pushing the weight back. I knew that I did not want to put shoes on the hind end, because that would increase the height of the hind end.

No Bar Shoe Here

The next logical step was to try something else.

Bob encouraged me to try something, since there was nothing to lose. A lame horse would not help his program. However, he could not afford to replace the animal. So, I proceeded to shoe King's front feet. I rejected the idea of a bar shoe on the right front, because I thought that I would concentrate first on lifting the left front. If the horse stepped in manure a bar would trap the material against the hoof. So on the right front I just attached a flat shoe.

Cushion Coming

Then, on the left front, I had to find the material that would give me the desired height of one inch without being too bulky or causing the shoe to slide around on this big horse. Fortunately, Bob had just gotten some conveyer belt rubber, the rubber that is used in large machinery which transfers materials up from one floor to the next. He said that he had intended to lay it down in the stallion's stall, to help prevent any more sores and provide him some cushion for standing. It proved to be the perfect material for this pad. Cutting through this stuff takes time because the material had steel wire reinforcement in it.

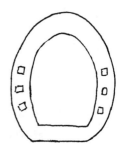

**A
Patient
King**

Sometimes there is a point of desperation that we all reach, and in this case I had to be willing to try it and go right ahead.

Admittedly, what I was about to do looked bizarre. People don't like bizarre and they don't like standing around listening to the rationale behind methods that seem strange. However, observations and my intuitive understanding were beginning to fit a pattern as I concentrated on analyzing the horse's balance.

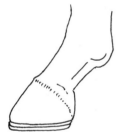

As I completed the task, I was impressed again with this giant of an animal. He had the capacity to hurt us all, but he chose to cooperate. Gazing up at King, I really appreciated his patience. We walked him around after attaching the shoes, giving the workman time to lay the rubber matting down in the stud's stall before we returned him.

**The
Mountain
Moved**

Walking beside this beast, my thoughts turned to daydreams . . . seeing scenes in movies where there were knights in armor, riding about on horses this big—they had to be this big so they could carry the weight. We were passing through the court of King Arthur, and his Round Table. Suddenly my daydream came to an abrupt halt when the mountain decided to move beside me.

For a moment I thought I was in real trouble, but King only jumped in place. It was impressive to see and enjoy this horse's gentleness. As I walked him back to his prison, I asked

Bob to call me and let me know of his progress. Then, driving away, I knew I was on the verge of solidifying my theory on the pressure points.

An Emotional High

Nothing matches the flood of excitement on the edge of discovery. The emotional high sent me home to analyze the theory further. Next evening, I got a call from Bob saying something had happened and I should come see it. I pressed him for more information, but he insisted on my coming out to see for myself. So I made arrangements to be out there early the next morning, before my first appointment.

A Sound Horse

That was one troubled night for me. I was so tied up with excitement and anticipation, I had to give up any hope of sleeping. When I arrived at the stable, a big grin lit Bob's face. I knew that the news must not have been too bad, and, sure enough, it wasn't. In fact, the sight was unbelievable. The left knee was no longer round. It looked just like the right knee. Bob said, "You were right. It was swollen all this time because he had been putting all his weight on the left front leg. Also," he went on, "the abcess is not seeping as much fluid." I warned him that it was still too early to be certain. Amazingly, the abcess cleared up in two weeks and never occurred again. The horse still suffered from the damage inside the coffin bone area, but he was now sound. Call it a fluke, or whatever you want, but the greatest success of all was the new stall Bob built for the stallion after two weeks, allowing this gentle giant to finally leave his prison once and for all.

Dear Tony,

Although I'd have liked to thank you personally, this letter will have to do for now.

Your contribution to the program and overall success of our recent Convention is most appreciated. The thoughts and skills you shared with the group were most valuable. I am sure that everyone who saw your work or heard you speak has been inspired to better themselves and their practice of farriery. This is the "bottom line", after all.

Thanks again, from me and from all who profited by your being there.

Sincerely,
Walter E. Taylor, President
American Farrier's Association

Chapter 4

Small Fry's Story

"If you can get him comfortable, I want him to live out his days teaching my son."

Small Fry's owner, Roy, was a good friend of mine. In fact, we grew up together. When we were young teenagers, we both started to rodeo, and ride junior bulls. At that time, Roy rode Small Fry and I rode Sonnyboy, my Palomino.

We used to meet at ropings and trail ride after we were done. Both Roy and I thought that we each had the best looking horses.

An Island Bred Horse

Small Fry not only played an important part in Roy's life, but mine as well. When Sonnyboy would get hurt, Roy would let me ride Small Fry to compete. Small Fry was actually an island bred horse. We Hawaiians have our own breed of horse. Old paniolas who worked the ranches claimed that the island breed consists of Spanish Barb mares, Thoroughbreds, Morgans and Hackney ponies. It may be difficult to imagine how versatile these little horses were. They could jump, chase cows, and carry 300 pounds on their backs. Yet, the average size for a horse was 14 hands. Back then, we did not consider size a factor when calling them horse or pony. To be fair, most of these animals were not what you would call halter-class material, but that is a matter of how one rides the head. Ha!

A Victim To Time

Small Fry fell a victim to time. When Roy started to outgrow him, the horse went on the market. Small Fry ended up on a rental string—not a very good life for a former star. Roy knew he was going to regret selling Small Fry to the stables, but he had an opportunity to buy a younger, and faster, quarter horse. One couldn't blame him for that. Roy was becoming one of the best ropers around and he needed a good horse.

Memory took me back to the day that Roy and I were in a big rodeo competition. We were both entered in junior calf roping. Unlike most friendships, winning or losing was not important. We both wanted the other to do well. Roy and I had just attended a clinic the week before, given by a professional calf roper, and we were eager to try out our new training.

When one is the first to go, there is a lot of pressure. Well, I was lucky—I was not first. In fact, I was last. There were eight of us young calf ropers. When Roy had his turn, he rated the fastest time for the juniors, 17 seconds. This was a great time. We were in a very good arena that

Memories

**Superstar
Roper**

allowed open space for the cattle to run. So, as confident as I could be, I knew that Sonnyboy was the fastest horse out of the chute and that he would be on this calf in no time. All I would have to do would be rope the calf and tie its legs. However, there was one factor I left out.

Already I was lifting weights for strength training, so I could hoist the calf off the ground and flank it onto its side. This was the new method I had learned. As Sonnyboy left the box, I was on target and caught the calf. I knew that if I could just tie its legs perhaps I would be done in 15 seconds. In those days I was using a lot of rope so I had to run down the rope a fair ways. As I got to the calf, I felt the superstar status take over in my mind. I could hear the praises and feel the pats on the back I was going to receive. Now this situation couldn't be better, the calf was cooperating. As I reached to lift the calf and throw him down on his side, I didn't bank on one factor. The calf was light. As I grabbed the animal I hoisted him up in the air, pulling him close to my chest and abruptly lost my superstar roper status. It was replaced by superstar comedian. I had pulled the calf up too high and fallen over backward.

**Superstar
Comedian**

All I wanted to do was crawl in a hole and die. What made everything worse as I lay there with the calf on my chest, was that both the calf and I were too embarrassed to get up. Needless to say, I lost, but the lesson in humility was worth the price.

All this came to mind one day, when I got a call from the military base that had Small Fry on the rental string. Many of these bases experience constant change of command. The confusion leaves people guessing all the time. The officer told me they were going to put three horses down. They wanted me to pull off their shoes, a sort of confirmation of their final fate. I accepted the job.

Fatal Confirmation

The work needed to be done in two days. That wasn't much time to dispose of a horse, but the military always acted that way. From earlier experiences I knew that these horses must have some very serious problems. At the bases, the men trail ride these horses as recreation. Most of the workers at the barn were young soldiers who didn't know much about horses.

As I arrived, all the horses were tied up at the metal fencing, saddled and ready for the day's adventures. For some reason, most military bases build their barns in the least likely spot. This base was no exception. The barn was on the side of a hill. Mud was a big factor from the constant rain that this area always experienced. The base dealt with the mud by building concrete stalls for the horses. This made it easy for them to wash away mud and manure. They simply hosed off the floor with water.

Mud, Rain, And Concrete

I headed to the office to see the person in charge only to learn he was in the back behind the barn. Among the three horses tied up there I saw Small Fry. The sergeant explained to me

43

Guilt To Come

that these were the three horses to be put down. The men had succeeded in finding a home for one of the horses, but Small Fry and the other were going.

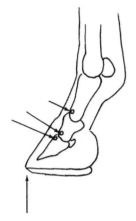

Inside, I knew that when Roy heard that Small Fry had been put down, he would feel guilty for the rest of his life. A few weeks before this job we had gotten together to reminisce. My friend remembered how beautiful Small Fry and Sonnyboy had been in our eyes. Back then we didn't know any better.

Roy said, "Today I look at Small Fry's pictures, and he looks like a close cousin to a donkey." But I knew having Small Fry go down this way would hurt him, so I did some fast talking and I bought Small Fry for $100. It was worth it to save him from this fate. Actually, I regret not having the space for the other horse who was put down.

Massive Case Of Ringbone

In this situation, it was the people, their riding habits, and their stable conditions that contributed to the horses' problems. Who would like to stand on concrete for up to 16 hours a day—on a good day? If it rained too much, then the horses would be in for 24 hours. The trails that they rode were military, made for vehicular traffic, and a lot of these riders felt like real cowboys when they rode the range running these horses at a full gallop. All of these conditions sometimes combined to create a massive case of ringbone. That was Small Fry's problem.

A vet friend of mine, Dr. Patrick Calla-han, used to say, "When you find calcium build up on the bone and in the joints, you will also see arthritis." Dr. Pat taught me well. I put Small Fry on some strong B complex vitamins, because Dr. Pat believed this would help blood circula-tion of the horse. It worked very well with Small Fry. Rubbing the affected area with linament and applying pine tar on the coronary band—to speed up any delayed healing—also worked well.

Dr. Pat Taught Well

I raised Small Fry's heels about 3 degrees, to 57 degrees. I put a rocker toe shoe on the front feet, but in making this shoe, I found that bevel-ing the outside edge of the whole shoe made the inside of the shoe the weight bearing surface. This helped to eliminate any wall pressure when the horse turned. I also added cushion pads to his front feet and used regular shoes on the hind feet.

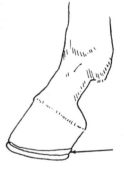

Let me elaborate on the beveled shoe a little more. It is important to avoid giving the animal any obstruction in the turns. Otherwise, one will find that the animal starts twisting his leg more to try to execute a turn. This creates more soreness in the leg.

Avoid Obstructing Or Start Twisting

Small Fry responded to treatment. The rest should be obvious. Small Fry became sound enough to be ridden by both Roy's child and my little girl. It did Roy's heart good to have Small

Worth It All

Fry back and it felt good knowing that I was able to help. When Roy said "If you can get him comfortable, I want him to live out his days teaching my son," I knew that the risk I took buying Small Fry was worth all of the money, time and effort that I had spent.

Chapter 5

Jim's Story

"He is going for lion meat because he is dangerous to ride!"

A. P. MASSIE

The stories from this chapter on have more questions in them for the reader to answer. Start thinking about solutions before I give my answers.

A Church Organization

It's hard not to be sympathetic when listening to a really sad story. This one came by phone from a church organization. The woman counselor from the church was polite as she asked if I knew of anyone interested in buying a chestnut gelding they had just purchased as a companion for another horse, like a babysitter. When I asked her how much they wanted for the horse, she responded "$300." This didn't sound like a bad price, considering how much horses were selling for at that time. However, a good price usually comes equipped with a good reason so I asked her what was wrong with this horse.

A Rearing Horse

Why were they selling the animal? Things got bizarre quickly. They were selling the horse because he was rearing. People were becoming afraid to ride him. This sounded logical to me. There are too many good, quiet horses to spend time trying to contend with a bad one. Even so, it was clear that there was more to the story.

In my profession one becomes a good investigative reporter, always searching for all the facts of the story. Another important factor in the sale was lameness.

What kind of lameness prompts a horse to

rear up when carrying a rider? Write out possible answers and compare them with the following explanation.

I arranged for an appointment to see the horse and then called my brother Moses to tell him the good news. He might be buying a horse. Moses thought I was crazy but we started to work on the theory as partners anyway. I would supply the mental groundwork and he would do the labor. As it turned out, Moses had the better job. Incidentally, it was Moses' idea to call the new technique and philosophy Proper Balance Movement (P.B.M. for short).

Moses' Idea: Call It P.B.M.

As Moses and I approached the church camp, we saw a herd of horses standing around tied up wearing their saddles. Voices of people nearby laughing and having fun filled our ears. People go to bed all over America dreaming about recreation on beaches like these under tall pines. The stable area, however, was cramped. A woman named Carmen ran the place.

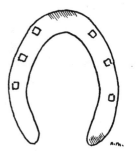

We had six horses to shoe there, so Moses and I finished our work before we looked at Jim. The animal looked appealing. He even appeared sound when Carmen brought him up to me. I examined him closely. He was a quarter horse— nothing spectacular, but very attractive just the same. Carmen put it bluntly, "If no one takes him, he is going for lion meat, because he is dangerous to ride!"

Zoos welcomed fresh horse meat for the

lions any day. Jim was too nice a horse to go that route.

Carmen offered the information that he was nine years old. I examined Jim's mouth to see if my estimation was the same, and we agreed. When I asked about the lameness, Carmen offered me x-rays. This was obviously not the woman who had called me.

Do you see the emerging pattern?

X-Rays Show A Spur

The answer is navicular. From what I had seen and heard, the horse was experiencing a wither or back problem but the x-rays showed a definite spur on the lower side of the left front foot. The right front was said to have some signs of injury also. This pattern explains the rearing.

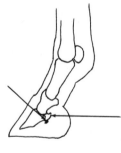

I directed Moses to mount the horse in the camp's little ring. The area was all sand, as you might have guessed from its beachfront location. While observing the horse's movement at a walk, the signs of obvious lameness started appearing. Jim began to bob his head up and down. Moses stopped the riding and I brought the horse to the truck. Sitting back and looking at him, I noticed a distortion, an overdeveloped left shoulder.

What should I do next? I decided to raise Jim's right front but the circumstances made it difficult to decide how much. Eventually, the most practical course was to check for a slight change in what I could do that day. In order to get a fair assessment of how much height I would need to level Jim, he would have to stand on fairly solid ground. This place had nothing but sand.

Since no one had been riding the horse, and since he had not been shod, Jim was an ideal candidate for an experiment. I attached only the right shoe and stepped back to watch for any change or reaction while Moses remounted for another ride.

One Right Shoe

Moses wasn't eager to test the horse's patience, but it was part of our partnership deal. Under the agreement Moses would provide the muscle and I would take the aspirins that come from making the brain perform in an unfamiliar fashion. For men in our business this was a reasonable division of labor.

As Jim started around, I discerned a slight difference in his movement. By that time I was starting to develop my eye—I saw movement a lot quicker. Watching Jim, I identified changes. He still maintained a slight limp but I noticed that he also started throwing the left front out forward more than he had been earlier. Jim was also beginning to show signs of wanting to rear so I stopped Moses before anything happened to him.

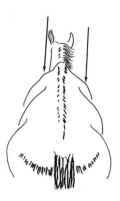

As Moses approached me, I asked for his evaluation. He could feel a freer motion but it was hard to tell without a saddle.

An Offer To Buy

When I asked Carmen how much they wanted for the horse, she said that the church had paid $300 for Jim and simply wanted the same amount for him. I didn't have the $300 available, so I turned to Moses and said, "Buy the horse." Using the charm so characteristic of brothers, he replied, "You're crazy!"

Pouring on the diplomacy myself, I told Moses that if I did not succeed in making this horse sound in six weeks, I would buy the horse from him, adding interest. Of course, I didn't say how much interest. Moses arranged to pick up the horse on the weekend.

Spurs On The Navicular

As we drove away, we began discussing what we had just done and were planning to do. The trouble seemed to be spurs on the navicular bone, a problem never cured up to that time. Of course very little research on the subject had been done either.

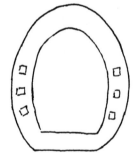

Buying Jim was a crazy idea, but I hated to see the horse go for lion meat.

As far as shoeing was concerned, everything was pretty standard. Normal practice dictated applying barshoes. The farrier has a choice of egg butt bar or raised bar shoe. An egg butt bar shoe has the shape of an egg and covers the buttress of the foot. A raised butt shoe has the bar sitting on top of the shoe so that there is no contact with the frog or heels. Pads function as shock absorbers eliminating concussion.

Something about the theory kept pricking at my mind, raising major doubts. It was difficult for me to believe what I was told. According to conventional wisdom, "Navicular's greatest

A Prickly Theory

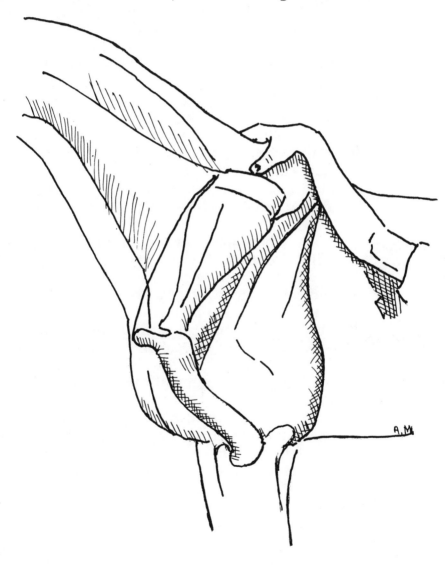

enemy is concussion." It simply didn't make sense to me to eliminate concussion by adding more metal to the shoe, even with more pads.

I had to question everything. That is always the first rule for a radical. I wasn't trying to prove the theory wrong, but I needed to fully understand why we put on these shoes. While making these investigations, I started looking for another way.

Pads And Plastic Shoes

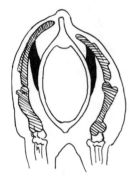

I considered pads and plastic shoes. It appeared that the most effective way to eliminate concussion was to find a shoe that would give total shock reduction within itself. This should work much better than adding metal.

When Moses brought Jim home, he was still convinced I was crazy, but deep down inside, he knew he could help Jim. I examined the horse on level ground. Putting my hand upon his shoulder blades near the withers, I was able to approximate that the difference in length was one and a half inches. This measurement, one and one half inches, tells the thoughtful observer how much to lift the horse.

Moses had also collected x-rays. After carefully examining the x-rays, I called the vet to see if he could provide any more background than the church had given me. He told me the same thing, the navicular was bad. I also opted to keep Jim off drugs because he seemed to have no pain when he just walked around.

Jim's ability to walk without pain seemed strange to me. In fact, it seemed so strange I became increasingly certain I needed more information to help him. The one inch lift wouldn't solve everything by itself.

Make a note and memorize this important lesson. Never radically raise a sound horse's legs. The procedure is exclusively a last resort for horses with no other alternative. I could risk experimenting because the horses coming to me were hopeless. They had failed to respond to all conventional treatments and I was a last chance stop on the way to dinner at the lion house in the zoo.

A Last Chance Stop

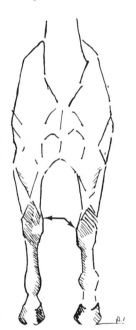

In the addition of one inch, it was important to find a way not to add too much weight to the horse's other leg. Therefore I applied a one quarter inch shoe on the left front foot and one quarter of an inch leather rim pad and a plastic shoe that was three quarters of an inch in width. Finally, I added a metal one quarter of an inch shoe. All this went on the right front.

The combination sounds like a lot, but actually fits quite nicely. Also, it was not all that heavy.

Now to consider the possible causes of the injury. What if there was a pressure point in the horse's foot, created by the uneven length? Could this be eliminated by rebalancing the front legs? The combination padding and shoeing would tell.

Painfully Slow Progress

Jim's progress was painfully slow. Each delay shot another hole in hopes the horse would heal quickly and brought home the big chance we had taken buying him. As much to keep our own hopes up as to speed recovery through exercise, Moses started riding Jim.

Jim had learned rearing so that he would not have to work. Although he had reason to be shy about being ridden at the beginning, now it became merely an excuse. While he was lame, when Jim's left front foot hit the ground, the compression would irritate the navicular bone. The irritation was increased by the weight of the rider and saddle.

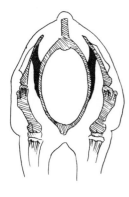

It took Jim three weeks to become sound. Eventually, he started to accept being ridden and he is now being ridden as a rope horse. There is no pain but this was no miracle.

All I had succeeded in achieving was the elimination of the constant strain on the pressure point on Jim's navicular bone. Eventually, this allowed any irritation and weakness to heal.

Some will call this treatment a bill of goods. How can any procedure be acceptable without first appearing in scientific journals with long experimental histories?

That kind of scientific rigor is slow and expensive. The only ways such scientists can know certainly that one bone is longer than another therefore causing a length problem or that a muscle is causing the stretch or perhaps the spine is twisted is to dissect the animal. You can imagine what that does for repeat business.

Sound Horses, Not Journal Reports

As a horseshoer I need to make horses sound. Ninety-five percent of my customers want sound horses, not reports from theoretical journals. The scientific data I actually need fits into my diary or my head.

As Jim progressed, his rearing stopped and he learned to become a satisfactory roping horse. Moses and I were so wrapped up in Jim's progress and concern for any recurrence of navicular or other lameness symptoms, we had not noticed that there was someone watching us as well.

A Perfect Horse For Danny

A man named Dan had also liked Jim, but he was not an accomplished rider—much less a roper. Jim, when healthy, was a perfect horse for Danny. Eight weeks after we purchased Jim, Danny made an offer to buy the horse.

What a shock! I told him about Jim's navicular problem, but it didn't bother him. Danny had been watching us make this horse sound. Even after I explained to him that we could not guarantee how long Jim would stay sound, he maintained that for as little riding as Jim would be getting, he would be O.K. Nothing would scare this man out of buying Jim.

As I was getting ready to quote a price, Moses interrupted me with a reminder that I

Rescued From The Lions had never paid him the promised money for Jim. That gave Moses the upper hand and he took $800 dollars on the spot.

Perhaps this does not sound like very much, but for eight weeks work plus rescuing Jim from the lions, making him sound enough to take his new owner trail riding and chase a cow or two, I would say that everyone got a good bargain, but me. Moses took all the money.

Danny had the horse and I—well, all that I took
home was a headache.

Jim and Danny had a great time together.
I kept on working on him, actually working him
down to just a quarter inch difference in length
between the two front feet. It was an important
lesson for me, because it helped shape my thinking about using wedge pads, bar wedge pads,
plain pads, and rim pads. Most of the horses that
I work on today with problems related to compression and concussion are better off for what I
had learned with Jim. This philosophy works
well when a horseshoer remembers: the lighter
the better.

**The
Lighter,
The
Better**

The Future Takes Shape

Jim's case shaped my future as a horse-shoer. I had realized at the time that if any research was to occur for the benefit of the horse, I was going to have do the work on my own. Jim also taught me that navicular was not as bad as most people thought it was. There are many factors, and I realize that not every horse would respond to my treatment. Yet, to be able to bring back a few and give them more years of fun, use and freedom from pain certainly is well worth the effort.

Compression, Not Concussion

Jim's case also helped me understand why, in some situations, the bar shoe is not effective. Also, it was instructive that compression was the major factor in his case—not concussion. He helped me discover another type of navicular which I will explain later in another book. This discovery led to a shoeing technique that works. No one has all the answers but anyone can look for them. Then, as each person learns a part and the pieces begin fitting together, the excitement mounts. Suddenly new theories form and the world changes forever.

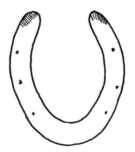

Chapter 6

Balance The Horse

What about the natural horse?
What changes does he undergo?

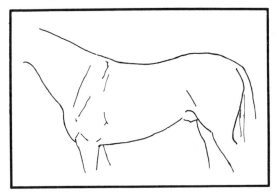

8. Desired Back

What is the natural horse's conformation, that is, its conformation in its natural state? When a horse is born, the colt must adapt its muscle structure to match its native surroundings, whether natural or man made. The environment may allow running free in pasture or may require confinement in a small stall or paddock.

In the years that I have been studying horses, I have seen the physical changes a horse goes through once it has been captured from the free environment of pasture and then confined to a small enclosure, whether a pen or a stall. Changes in feed, or other changes in the horse's

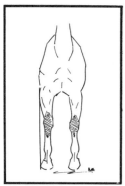

11. Side Balance

Pens And Stalls Limit Motion

diet, also affect the horse's development. Surprisingly, changes could be detected in the horse's hoof structure, as well.

Running free allows the horse to walk on different surfaces. These surfaces are always beneficial to the horse's needs. Taking a horse out of that environment leads to exercise on a consistent surface, which, in many cases, increases the constant wear of the horse's hooves. Also with horses kept in a smaller area, normally the animal stands with its full weight upon its legs. Pens and stalls limit motion and add to compression of the hooves. After many years of study, I found that, in a good many cases, when horses change environment from pasture to confinement, the hoof size will actually decrease for a while. Later, the hoof size will increase again as its physical body, internally and externally, adapts to the environment. This decrease of hoof size is a direct result of the hoof receiving greater compression from the bone weight and muscle weight. For a young horse, this pressure is constantly increasing, due to weight gain and loss of the free mobility the horse once had.

I became aware of these changes when I was working in Hawaii as a teenager, helping my father. Ranch horses that were just running wild appealed to my father who would buy them. These animals would come to us solid as rocks. Although their hooves were always in bad shape, the width was always good. I would find horses that always had substantial heels. They would be upright and be very strong boned. I used to think that when these horses showed signs of changes in the texture of hooves, and changes in growth patterns, they were responding to wearing shoes for the first time. Only horses that are never ridden could keep their natural conformation.

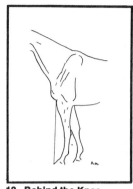

12. Behind the Knee

It is difficult to break new ground when professionals already have an answer for everything. Most people prefer to be traditionalists and that is a hard habit to break. However, what many people today fail to realize is that every answer that we have, and are comfortable with, was correct in the context in which it was sought. These answers were found by people who had seen where the conditions had changed, and found new answers. Since conditions are always changing, new answers are always needed. However, these new answers do not prove the old answers wrong, they merely show how the conditions have changed.

A Hard Habit To Break

Horses are not perfect as they are found in nature. They are only perfect as they are found in each horseowner's mind and heart. However, colts that grow up in a natural environment, and are left to roam in pasture, don't usually acquire several common problems. Only rarely will one find a free-roaming horse with a swayed back (this is where the conformation of the back has a downward bow in the middle). Even though one will find horses out in pasture with large bellies, their backs are rarely bowed. This is because a horse that has a swayed back has its abdominal

Imperfect Horses

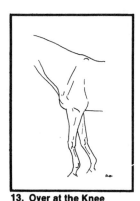

13. Over at the Knee

muscles pulling the back down through gravitational pull. Anything heavy will succumb to the earth's gravitational pull. The roaming horse does not have a sway back because the animal spends most of its time lifting its head up and down constantly. Horses that graze have very little time to look up, if you know what I mean. This up and down motion of the head forces the back to rise upward, thereby pulling the stomach away from the earth's gravitational pull, strengthening the back muscles and tightening the stomach muscles.

Natural Versus Ridden

The stance of the natural horse is also somewhat different from that of the ridden horse. Because the animal carries its own weight, it will have a greater tendency to stand underneath itself and be balanced. It is also noteworthy that horses raised on hills and mountains develop differently from those roaming on flat ground.

A Surprising Discovery

In recent years there has been an influx of tendon problems with colts. Interestingly, almost all the colts that I saw with contracted tendons were stall or confined paddock babies. Of course, there were a few pasture babies with this problem too. It was surprising to discover that most of the babies had one leg worse than the other. The standard shoeing procedure was always to cut the heels down. Actually, in many cases this made things worse. I used to feel bad about having to follow instructions, because I saw a lot of babies stop liking me and get upset every time I came near them. The colts would feel fine when

I would get there to trim them, but when I finished trimming them, using the standard method of chopping off heels, the babies would walk off lame. In many cases they would be stepping on their toes. There had to be another solution.

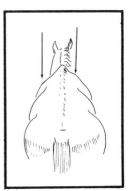

14. High Right Shoulder

Once I was treating a baby that was a twin. She was the only survivor, and she was born fine. Her birth was in the winter, so she spent a great deal of time inside. There were no texts at hand explaining how to raise a surviving twin, so I treated both the filly and the mare as normal. Later, it became apparent that I had helped to create a calcium-phosphorus imbalance in the baby's system. This caused the tendons to contract. It was explained to me that this occurs when the bones grow faster than the tendons and ligaments. Having the foal penned in without a lot of movement did not improve her condition. She was too small for shoeing to make much of a difference, and casting her was out of the question, so I saw no solution.

Too Small To Shoe

Then, one day during the spring, I saw the filly do something that I would never have thought was possible. Her living quarters consisted of a stall, and a good size paddock with a small ditch in it. I saw the filly standing down in this ditch with her front feet up on the bank. While her mother was eating grass nearby, she was actually stretching her tendons using the bank. On top of the hill was a telephone pole with a guide wire. The owner of the place had built a board fence around the guide wire so the

Self-Healing

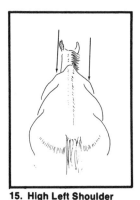

15. High Left Shoulder

horses would not be exposed to risk from accidentally running into it. Well, during the transition from spring to summer, when the filly's coat was shedding, the filly would put her rear end up against the fence. Keeping her butt uphill, she'd sit on the fence stretching her legs. She actually straightened out on her own, helping herself. Her feed program had been changed, and now the angle in her pastern was being straightened. This was a far cry from having her ankles falling over.

Stiffness

Constantly cutting off the heels means the animals have to shift their weight to the hind legs. This places more pressure in the hocks of the back legs creating stiffness. Consequently, the stiffness was due to compensation for the pain of the front legs, trying to force the tendons and ligaments to stretch. People ask me all the time about the conditioning of horses in the wild. Sometimes we forget that in the wild horses live by the rule of survival of the fittest. Predators kill the unhealthy horses.

Club Feet

When I was working on wild horses from the ranches, I never ran into a horse with contracted tendons. However, there were horses with club feet. Once, it seemed that a horse with a club foot had a defect. Now it is clear that the horse with two club feet has a defect. What is called club footed in horses with only one club foot, is not that at all. The formation of the club foot results from a deformed coffin bone. A deformed coffin bone develops in a young horse when the tendons which stretch down to the foot do not develop completely on the short leg (front or hindquarters). Contact with the ground is made with the front of the foot. The heel tends to grow while the toes receive unnatural wear and the shock from compression produces uncommon stress on the coffin bone.

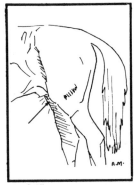
17. Stifle

No horse is equally balanced from side to side. This is true for bone as well as muscle. With careful observation, several inequalities can be found in the conformation of every horse. A horse has one leg that is longer or shorter than the other three. If the leg is shorter, one heel grows upward, adding height to the leg. If the leg is longer, the heel of that foot is lower and allows more toe growth on that hoof. This lessens height to the leg. The mane over the withers will always fall to the lower side.

Down Goes The Mane

In the hind end, it is not as easy to determine the lower side, since there is no mane to make it obvious. Instead, the longer leg can be identified by the shape of both sides of the hip, and also the stride of the hind legs. In motion, a front leg that is longer will generally have to shorten. A shorter front leg will have to lengthen. In the hind end it is just the opposite. The longer leg in the hind end will lengthen under the body and the shorter leg will shorten its stride outside of the body. This is all done to insure balance naturally.

The Longer, The Lower

It is important to note that the longer leg in the front will almost always have the lower heel. There are exceptions, which will be covered

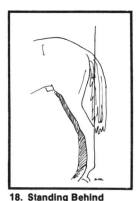

18. Standing Behind

Hip Up, Hind Down

in another book, along with the reasons. The lower heel allows the toe of the foot to contact the ground sooner. This motion brings about minimal arc, which allows the shoulder blade to drop down and back. The short leg will almost always have the higher heel. This increases the angle, making the flight of the foot higher. Further, this allows the shoulder blade to come up higher and equalize the balance from side to side.

Now the hind end motion is different. The longer hind leg, because of the hip joint, will always have to move inward under the stomach in order for the hip to level off. The hip will go up so the hoof comes off the ground, then the hip will drop to level when the hoof strikes the ground. The shorter hind leg will go down when the hoof leaves the ground. Then it will come up when the hoof strikes the ground. The motion is down and then up to level. This is a guide to use in order to determine motion.

Chapter 7

Debby's Story

**"I know he is going lame, but
no one else can see it!"**

A Young Horse In Training

Sunday can be a busy time for horse-shoers. It is the night most people use to discuss the success or failure of their weekend ventures.

One Sunday there was a phone call from Debby. Her voice was filled with concern. Debby had a very young horse she had been training hard for dressage. He was pretty good, too. The problem that was alarming Debby was a feeling more than anything else. The performance of the horse was great, he would place in the ribbons, but she had detected a movement problem.

As Debby continued talking about her horse, a familiar reaction set in. Perhaps this woman was a little bit paranoid, or, possibly, she was not willing to admit that she was doing something wrong. Were these symptoms leading up to another demand for a miracle cure? Debby felt the young horse was going to become lame and that no one else could see what she was talking about. It was hard to see how the situation could be so serious if no one else saw any problem. When I challenged her perceptions, she became defensive. Now it really looked like she was off her rocker!

To start, I asked her who had looked at the horse. Debby listed two vets, three trainers, and the judge at the last horse show. The scores on this horse's tests were good. The judge liked the horse and had told her that she was overreacting. I began to sympathize with Debby. Here she knew something was going to happen, she went looking for help from the knowledgeable people

around her, and they wouldn't believe her. Perhaps it would help her and help the horse if she found one person who thought she was right.

Seeing A Horse's Movement

I arranged for us to meet Tuesday morning at 10 o'clock. This provided enough time to gather my thoughts together about what options were available for this situation. In those days, I was not trained well enough to fully see a horse's movement, so I knew I was a bit handicapped as well. Frankly, it was hard to know how much could be done if no one could see what problems she was talking about. The uncertainty made it harder to conceive how to check and analyze the horse's movement. What kind of shoe do you put

71

on a horse that has this problem? Is it a real problem or just a phobia on the owner's part? Back to the books I went, seeking out shoes that could be valuable in helping, or at least identifying, the situation.

Concern Over Interference

A.M.

Without knowing more about the full story, I had to assume several different problems. If the trouble was extension—the horse not being able to reach stride length needed for the proper forward motion—then the option was to lower the heels of the front feet, use a shoe that had some type of build up at the toe to increase the angle, or even a turn to a toe grab.

If the problem was not enough knee action, then I would have to figure out a way of making the horse snap its knee joint higher. This could be done by cutting only the toe off the front feet, allowing the heels to grow up higher. The solution would increase chances of the foot breaking over faster. A rolled toe shoe would work, if the toes were too long and the heel growth was lower. A shoe that had height at the heel would be appropriate in this case. Even a calk shoe could be used.

However, if the difficulty was in the hind end, then a whole new way of thinking would come into play. The first concern in this case would be possible interference between the front legs and the hind legs. Could the hind legs be coming up too far before the front feet could come off the ground? If so, then the hind legs would have to be reduced in speed and the front end sped up.

Now the options here are good: for the front use a rolled toe shoe, or a rocker toe shoe, as it is sometimes called. This can be used on the hind legs as well. One can also use a trailer on the outside of the shoes to help direct the desired breakover. A square toe shoe could also work.

Clearly, there was no shortage of options to use in this case. As I arrived at the barn, Debby was standing, grooming her horse. It was a gorgeous spring day and the setting could not have been better for what I was going to discover. The barn was small and private, no more than six stalls in an attractive, well kept surrounding. In fact we were the only ones present. Approaching the young horse, I suddenly realized that I had been so preoccupied with Debby's concerns, I had completely forgotten the horse had no shoes on.

Until then, I was expecting to arrive rather easily at an answer—decide the proper type of shoes to use. Now it would be necessary to analyze the horse's movement without shoes, find a difficulty that six people before me had not been able to find, and come up with an answer as well as a solution. Debby would insist upon knowing why the horse was going lame and learning what she needed to do to keep her horse healthy.

Debby was a tall woman, about six feet with brown hair and a great personality. She was a young professional and achievement-minded. Only one thing concerned me—she was a perfectionist. Perhaps because she had not been treated very well by my predecessors, I was going to have to convince her that I was doing more than jollying her for her money.

A Good Side, A Bad Side

The owner emphasized that I was the first horse professional interested in what she felt and suspected from riding her horse. It was as if she had finally found someone she could talk to openly. Debby sensed in her horse an insecure feeling, movement to the right. Also, there were times when the horse would execute a slight slipping of the left front in a turn.

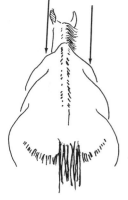

She had reached the conclusion that her horse had a good side and a bad side. He was better turning to the right but the motion was much more rigid. Turning to the left he was more supple, but he sometimes would fall into his turns prematurely. Debby judged that this difficulty pointed to the real problem.

Listening To Rider Terminology

While she was talking to me and grooming the horse, I was observing the horse's conformation. I really could not see anything that was obviously a cause or sign of a problem. As I listened to her explain her impressions in rider terminology, I had to control my reaction. Another disappointment, no easy answer. I began to wonder why God was picking on me.

The horse's legs were clean. There were no signs of soreness on the hooves. Debby said that she only rode on grass and the rings that she rode in were all soft. Scratch that theory. I asked her to walk the horse away from me and back to me. Then in front of me, from side to side, so that I could get a side view of the horse's movement— to see if there was an overreaching problem. No sign of any such problem. I was now seeing what everyone else was seeing, nothing out of the ordinary. This horse was level-headed and one could see this reflected in the manner in which he responded to whatever Debby asked of him.

Then Debby rode him bareback, so I could compare the motion with and without the rider's weight. Perhaps the problem was related to how she was riding him. She walked him away from me and then towards me. She cantered away from me, then towards me. There was no sign of any problem. Then I asked her to circle him, and to do some figure 8's. I was still unable to see anything wrong. However, I could sense now that there was something happening by the expression on Debby's face. Every time she felt the movement, I could see disappointment in her face. I tried hard to see what she was feeling, without success. Then, suddenly there was a breakthrough.

Rounding the far corner of the ring, as the horse had its left front leg in the air, Debby shifted her weight to adjust to the turn. The horse had to pivot sharply in order to maintain its balance, thus affecting the shoulder's motion. The horse stumbled, but this problem was not caused by the animal's toe striking the ground

Suddenly, A Breakthrough!

A Stumbling Horse

Debby Was Right

first. Somehow, it was as if the ground were not under the horse's foot. Evidently something was affecting this horse.

Debby's insight had been right. There were the makings of a serious problem. Of course, seeing the problem is not the same thing as finding the answer.

She started to bring the horse to me. As she did so, I noticed that the sun had been throwing great shadows on the riding ring. The sunlight shone through the trees and actually hit the horse in the chest area. I saw his knees and I couldn't believe my eyes. I was wearing glasses, so my first thought was that my eyes were tired. I had Debby get off her horse to confirm what I was seeing. We both saw the same thing.

I went back to my truck and got out my tape measure to gauge the hoof length of both front feet. They were the same. However when I measured the length of both front knees there was a difference of three quarters of an inch between the two. The right front leg was actually longer than the left. The discovery opened the way to design an action plan. Debby did not really have a lame horse, but the horse would go lame unless something were done.

Long Leg Discovery

The whole thing baffled me. How had the horse gotten that way? What could I do to change it? I decided the best way to handle a three quarter inch difference was to build up the short leg until both legs were level. There was no way of telling what effect the extra padding would have on the natural motion and balance. Debby agreed to let me shoe the horse's front feet, so I put a three degree pad on the left front. After that, the knees were almost level. I could feel my confidence grow. Then, I trimmed the hind feet. It was time to test the theory.

Nearly Level Knees

Debby remounted the horse and rode him about for me. Two separate entities were now reacting to the change in a positive manner. The rider could definitely feel the difference. The same drill that made the horse lose its balance was no problem. This time Debby was very happy with the performance.

It was too early to be certain of the cure. Adverse consequences might yet surface. Horseshoeing provides regular reminders not to take appearances at face value, because that can depreciate to rock bottom the next day.

Debby had definite plans for this horse. She was not going to change them after this success. I asked her to take it easy on him for a couple of days, and then to call me with a progress report, three days later.

Excitement And Fear

I was excited at how well the padding seemed to work, but there was still fear inside.

Three days later the phone rang. The voice froze me to my chair with fear. For a moment, it was tempting not to answer her. Curiosity won. Debby was ecstatic. The horse

Secure And Even

had been doing well. She said that he felt more secure and had evened up in his circling movements in both directions. This was music to my ears.

Distress And Disappointment

Of course, there was no reason to let her know I still had some doubts whether the padding was a complete solution. Enjoying her pleasure in our success, I asked her if she thought there would be other benefits. We had a grand time talking about the success, then she revealed to me that the horse's attitude had changed. Now, he always seemed ready to work. I cautioned her about doing too much with him too soon, but she assured me she had been careful to take everything into consideration. We agreed on a future schedule, then as I hung up, relief flooded through me.

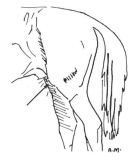

Another job well done, another happy customer.

Three weeks later, I heard from Debby again. This time, I heard distress on the phone. Her joy had turned to sadness and disappointment. The horse was lame.

Lame In The Hind Legs

This time, the lameness was not in the front legs, it was in the hind legs. This sounded crazy. After all, the horse was unshod behind. On the other hand, this could be the very reason. I told her that I would postpone an appointment and see her the next morning.

I arrived at 10 o'clock to find a very sad

Debby. Her dreams might be shattered if no reason for the problem could be found. The vet had identified the fact that the horse had a sore right hind stifle. I found the same thing, the horse would respond to even a light touch on the stifle.

A Horse With A Sore Stifle

After describing what I found to Debby, she opened her conscience to me, blaming herself for not listening to my warnings. When the horse had looked like he could work more, she pushed him harder. It was difficult to scold her for not listening to me.

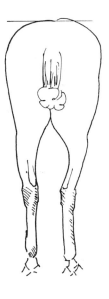

I could understand her decision.

Now it was important to understand why this soreness developed. I examined the horse's hind legs closely, because I realized that I did not pay attention to them when I saw the front legs the first time. I had been preoccupied with the front legs and I hadn't noticed that the horse had a higher hip on the right. This meant that the horse's whole right side was higher. But how could this be?

I examined the muscles inside of the hind legs, as well as outside the hind legs. There was a substantial difference in development. I asked Debby if she would take the horse to the vet's once more, to show the vet what I saw and to see if he could shed some light on this conformation.

The Whole Right Side?

Meanwhile, I suggested we shoe him when

A Disabled Car

he came back from the vet's. She agreed to do as I asked.

As I drove away, I was confused. Nothing had been said about whether padding the front left hoof was a possible cause of the soreness. Clearly, it had some effect.

The Underlying Cause

Traveling to the next appointment, I saw a car broken down on the side of the road. It had a flat tire. As I approached the car, preparing to pass it, I couldn't avoid noticing that the flat tire must have been on the right rear wheel. It was obvious from the way the rear bumper slanted.

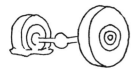

The disabled car opened my eyes to the underlying cause for lameness. The theory didn't come together all at once but at last I knew the direction my research would take.

Debby called back a few days later with news that she had received confirmation of what I had seen. However, there were no real answers for me. As we talked I explained to her that I thought I had an answer.

Weight To The Rear

We met two days later and I reexamined the horse.

Now I understood what had happened. I explained to Debby that the problem had been in the hind end originally. Therefore, when I lifted the front left, I forced more weight back onto the right hind.

The car with the flat tire helped explain what happened. To make the analogy work, a small tire substituted for the flat one. Pressure and strain on the larger tire on the opposite side would eventually cause something to burn out.

One Horse, One Unit

The horse taught me a valuable lesson. The entire horse is one unit.

Front End- Hind End Connections

Even though I was not being blamed for the lameness, I felt somewhat responsible for not identifying the problem earlier. This experience really enriched my understanding. Now, there was more to horseshoeing than putting on shoes. Debby and I agreed we should try to level the animal off by raising the left hind leg half an inch. The horse went sound in three days.

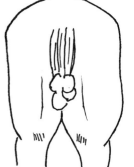

The front end of the horse is connected to the hind end of the horse. What the farrier does in front with shoeing and padding will affect what happens to the hind end. The reverse also applies. It should have been obvious that the left front was compensating for the right hind problem all along. So when I raised the left front, I made the right hind carry the load it was supposed to. The physical build left the right hind leg too weak, so the horse went lame.

Gut Feelings Confirmed

An owner or rider's gut feelings are overlooked in far too many cases. Everyone has been through this experience. I truly believe that the horseowner knows a horse better than anyone

The World Of Motion Shoeing

else. Most people can tell when a problem occurs in an animal's movement from on top of the horse's back. The real problem is putting that knowledge into words.

Debby's horse was also my introduction into the world of motion shoeing. The effects of riding can be critical as a contributing factor to lameness. When Debby got out of synch with the horse's balance, the movement problem occurred.

Chapter 8

Bojangles' Story

**"I have a problem. I need for you
and my vet to get together."**

When I am giving talks on my Proper
Balancing Movement philosophy, I often receive
requests to be more technical when I explain
things. Unfortunately, when I make my talks
more technical, then I see a lot of confused
people.

A.M.

Upper Body Conformation

This case demonstrates how upper body conformation can cause an animal's problem. To some degree, it doesn't matter what the specific problem is. But it is important to see how problems in the upper body can create symptoms in the legs and feet.

As a horseshoer, I can't take away calcium, replace the navicular bone, fix a damaged tendon, or work other, similar miracles. All a farrier can do is relieve stress and work on preventing any further damage. Horseshoeing has always been a means of dealing with problems after they have developed. Now, it's time to start developing before-the-fact shoeing—preventive maintenance.

Many considerations have to be balanced to gain an adequate look at the complete picture. First there is the normal flow of the horse's movement to consider. Then the introduction of the rider's movement on the horse's back deserves study. Also, it is important to analyze the compensation movement. I've spent the past five years showing people how to identify what they have been looking at and never seen.

Preventive Maintenance

I received a call from a woman who was very polite to me, so polite in fact that I was suspicious. When I asked her what her problem was, I heard silence. The silence told me that this must have been a very important phone call. She was trying to find diplomatic words to tell me that I was going to be put on trial.

At this point, the woman's vet knew her horse's problem. However, he wanted to find out what I knew about the problem and also what methods I knew for treating the horse. By this time, I was having some pretty good luck. Because of human nature, everyone is afraid to ask me questions—for fear that I might bite their heads off. Evidently word had not gotten out that I welcomed dialog with anyone. After all, that's how I gained the knowledge in the first place. Input from others also helps me know if I'm on the right track in my thinking.

I Don't Bite

Finally, the owner offered her reason for calling. Bojangles' problem was a left arthritic knee, so an appropriate time had to be worked out for the vet and me to meet. I was pleased about this opportunity. I suppose it could have been seen as insulting, but I was grateful for an opportunity to talk over my thoughts with a veterinarian. I knew this vet, but normally we were not able to get together. For the most part, his schedule was too busy. He treated not only horses, but dogs, cats, zoo animals, fish at the aquarium and even the sharks. So there were no thoughts of avoiding each other. This was more of a privilege than a meeting.

A Left Arthritic Knee

My ego enjoyed hearing that he wanted to know more of what I was doing as well. As I arrived at the barn holding Bojangles' stall, I met the owner. She was a stoic woman, tall and apparently a loner. She showed no interest in socializing with the barn full of people. Yet, there was about her an admirable air of class.

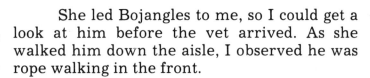
Rope Walking Observed

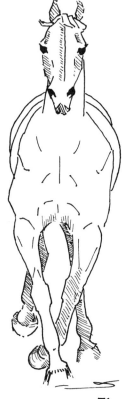

The Saddle Shift

She led Bojangles to me, so I could get a look at him before the vet arrived. As she walked him down the aisle, I observed he was rope walking in the front.

Drawing him closer to me, I could see that his left shoulder was much higher than his right. She lifted her saddle and placed it on his back.

Hints began taking shape in my mind.

As she withdrew, I walked Bojangles forward while I walked backwards in front of him myself. This way she could see exactly where the swing in his step was originating. I returned him back to her and she began saddling him.

Now rope walking, or tightrope walking as it is sometimes called, means a horse moves his front legs forward. The legs actually go toward the center of the body alignment. One front foot crosses in front of the other one. One foot is actually going straight while the other one is crossing over it.

Bojangles was a rope walker with an arthritic left knee. This pattern fits together so commonly the skilled observer will spot it regularly.

I also expected to find a characteristic pattern in the saddle. On rope walkers, the saddle will shift to one side. Keeping in mind that Bojangles had a left high shoulder and a low right side the reader should be able to predict

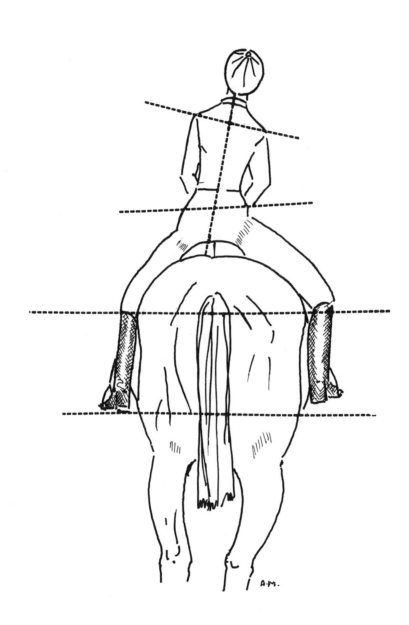

what kind of saddle placement I found and describe the characteristic rider action.

A Final Exam

As I was doing my final examination of Bojangles, the vet showed up. He was anxious about what I was doing, so I told him that I was just checking to see how the saddle fit. I unsaddled Bojangles, and asked Jane if she could take the horse down to the arena. There, we could watch the horse on the lead line. The vet also spotted the rope walking. He didn't know why the horse was moving that way. In fact, he was hoping I could shed some light on the situation. The vet knew I had been working on the movement of horses and its effect on lameness as part of my theoretical study.

As we stood behind the horse and watched him travel down the hill, I explained that the horse was actually taking the left front leg and throwing it in front of the right front. At the same time, the right front leg was going straight. When we were almost at the ring, I noticed something that had not been picked up before. The horse was favoring the left hind leg as well. This should have been obvious from the way he was walking.

The Effect Of Movement

At the ring, I directed Jane to make the horse walk left. When Bojangles began moving left the effect intensified. The left leg passed across the right front more demonstrably on the left circuit than when walking straight.

Horseshoers would automatically notice

that the left front hoof was taking on the pigeon toe look and rotating with the center of the toe pointing inward. The pressure now centered on the outside half of the hoof from the quarters to the heels.

The left hind hip also came forward. Consequently the lower leg was coming much more forward underneath the body as well. The toe was also twisting, rotating the left hock outward causing the center of the back toe to rotate inward—putting more weight on the outside half of the hind hoof.

At first, the vet had difficulty finding all these symptoms.

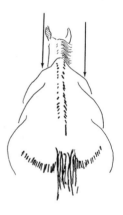

As Bojangles was led in the other direction, he showed signs of being more comfortable. In fact he could negotiate the turn better than he could from the left and there was more suppleness in his movement.

Doc wanted to know why one side worked better than the other. After reading this far the reader should know enough to explain.

We returned to the barn and I began my explanation. At this point, I was not accustomed to telling what I perceived. Generally, there were few people who knew what I was talking about. It was even harder to talk to Doc about the rider's point of view when he had never ridden a horse before. Still, I did the best I could.

A Narrow Chest And Shoulders

Let's get back to the facts. Bojangles' problem was the left front knee. There were also some signs that the left hind leg had a problem. The left shoulder was higher, and he rope walked.

Picture Bojangles' conformation. He was a narrow horse with little width between the chest and shoulders. Because he was actually higher in the hind end his head carriage was high. Horses that are higher in the hind end will carry their heads up in order not to fall head over heels forward with riders on their back. Bojangles was starting to become a little cow hocked, and his back was hollowing out. The stomach was lower to the ground. Normally, when the stomach muscles are taking over, that means the back muscles will begin to atrophy. Consequently the back weakens and the stomach strengthens.

Lack Of Chest Muscle

The principles behind rope walking are simple. Lack of chest muscle causes the animal to have a limited amount of stretch in the outward leg motion. The outward leg motion is what actually allows the leg to move forward. When a horse has a narrow chest, the shoulders, which have to level off for the horse to maintain balance, restrict the movement of the left front leg. This process creates the rope walk. Cross-leg motion pushes the shoulder blade back and downward. From this motion, the animal shortens muscle development which in turn, produces more constriction in motion.

90

Each problem compounds the next in the series.

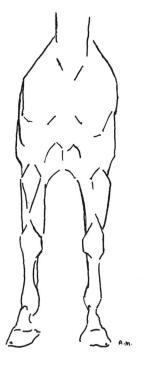

Muscles that constrict shorten both the distance that a leg travels, and also the time that the foot stays off the ground. When the foot makes contact too soon, it will strike the ground first with the toe, and then the heel. Red bruising at the white line of the toes of the hoof and compressed heels result from the hoof striking the ground too early. Premature contact of the hoof with the ground will increase the amount of concussion that travels up the front of the leg.

A Shortened Distance

Other problems arise from rope walking. The bones of the knee are actually grinding because of the inward motion. This rubbing of the bones in the joint produces a calcium buildup. The calcium buildup develops on the inside of the left knee rather than on the outside of the knee. The rope walking motion causes the knee to twist in and break over to the outside. Horseshoers find the outside heel ground down more than the inside heel on rope walkers, creating the pigeon toe look. The problem occurs on the left front more often than the right front.

Because of this inward knee motion, Bojangles could not actually take the left front leg completely to the outside of the body. Any time he tried to extend the left leg to the outside of the body, the left shoulder blade would stick straight up in the air. This would leave the shoulder exposed, making it vulnerable to being hit or pinched by the rider. If the left leg were to go

A Twisting Knee

Equal Distance For Stride

straight forward, breakover would be possible. The uneven length of both front legs would end up making the horse lose balance, thereby causing both the horse and rider to fall.

In order for the horse to balance both its own weight and the rider's weight with forward momentum, its legs must travel at an equal distance for stride. In a case of rope walking, one leg is too short to match the other. While rope walking, the horse actually appears to have both legs moving towards the inside. Actually there is only one leg moving inward. In Bojangles' case it was the left front. The right front leg was moving straight.

Weight Pressing Down

There are two reasons for this. If both legs moved inward in the same direction, the horse's movement would be like that of a person mixing salad in a salad bowl. If this were to happen, the animal would trip over its own legs and become dangerous. Secondly, if a horse wanted to shorten the distance that the front legs travel, the leg would have to swing inward or outward in order to move forward at an adequate length to maintain balance.

Bojangles' greater height in his hind quarters increased the amount of weight pressing down in the front legs. When a horse is higher in the rear it will be heavy on the forehand. The unevenness of the body height, from back to front, causes the difficulty in the horse's natural movement to grow worse when a rider's weight is added. When ridden, the horse must propel

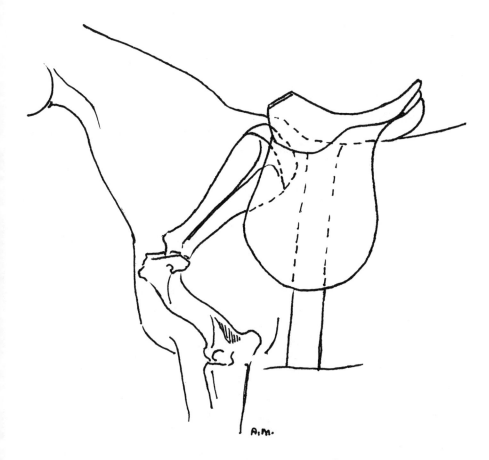

itself upward even higher in the front end in order to move forward with the extra weight on its back. As the horse propels itself upward, it will also land on the ground harder, which creates more concussion. This greater concussion creates a harder shock to the knee when it closes.

Shock To The Knee

The hollowed back and characteristic overdeveloped belly muscles reflect rider abuse.

When this kind of horse slopes downhill, the rider tends to fall forward with full weight on every stride. Because most riders who do this are unaware of what they are doing, they risk serious damage to the horse.

Risk Of Serious Damage

Riders have an inclination to distort their bodies to keep level. Often riders will dismount after a workout with backs sore from this distortion. I've heard some unbelievable excuses from riders who think they have sound reasons for riding this way. However, they are always shocked when they see themselves on video tape.

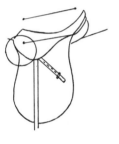

Now in Jane's case, I had her saddle up Bojangles, and take him back to the ring. Doc was so interested in our analysis, he called his office to have them refer calls to his partner for the next hour. As we walked behind Bojangles again, going down the hill, I quickly pointed out the difference in distance of the hind legs with a rider's weight on the back. Bearing the rider also caused the left front to swing inward more than it had before. Watching him move on the flat ground, we saw the same thing. An important part of the observation here was watching how the rider adjusted to the horse's body movement. Jane's body was tilted backward now. The small of her back was bowed, with her shoulders and head back. Her legs were straight and heels down. A good seat, but—and here's a big but—her balance was now in her hindquarters. With this posture, every time Bojangles

See The Rider Adjust

dropped his head, the rider's rigid body would be lifted forward out of position.

Tripping

Bojangles tripped once when this happened. When his left front foot was in the air and Jane was unseated at that moment, Bojangles' left leg came down to the ground prematurely. Then his toe hit first, snapping the knee back faster, causing a shock and pain. When I pointed this out to Jane, she agreed that she was heavy in the hind. She had thought he was also rear heavy. Jane's analysis was correct, but the root of the problem was conformation.

Falling

Jane was also falling on Bojangles' right front shoulder, causing him significant pain. In part, this was due to his right shoulder being lower, but the biggest problem was Jane's compensation. Her reaction was to throw her weight on to the left cheek of her buttocks. This pressure would now make Bojangles bring up his left hind leg under the body in order to support the rider, as well as raise his hip higher to prevent Jane from falling off toward the left rear.

Talking

After I pointed these things out, Doc was able to see what I was talking about. He asked for my solution, so I gave it to him.

As we once more walked back up the hill, Doc asked me, "In how many horses have you found this uneven development? How much of the horse population?"

Don't Make Waves

I told him all horses. Here came the look again—he thought I was out of my head. I explained, "Doc, there are some horses that are near perfect, and there are some that are really off. The most that I have ever added to balance a horse was two inches. That was a lot.

"Maybe I have to work on three of every ten horses to some degree. Not every horse has to be balanced. I only balance a horse when the animal is dead lame or needs a minor movement adjustment. When the horse is sound—don't make waves!" I went on to tell Doc that many horses were either lame or needed help in their movement because of the particular riding style of their owners. Many riders feel that their horses can do any type of riding. Most often, riders also neglect to take the time to build these animals up physically for the work. The reason even more horses are not lame today, is that many horseowners have found the right conformation horse for the type of work that they need done. Also, it helps that many are not doing too many different types of riding with one horse.

As we arrived up at the barn, I told Doc what I was going to do. I estimated that Bojangles was an inch off between the two front legs. So I was going to lift the right front leg three quarters of an inch.

Doc looked at me with a pessimistic stare. I wasn't offended. I had been down that road before.

I also was going to put a pommel pad on the horse's withers, to raise the saddle up front so that it would not sit on the withers.

When I was finished, we took Bojangles down to the ring. We tested him first without a rider or saddle. Jane moved Bojangles out on the lead line, and the rope walking was now minimal. I asked for a walk, trot, and canter in both directions. When he finished cantering, the rope walk, and even the lameness, completely disappeared. The movement was even.

No Rider, No Saddle

Next we put Jane on the horse's back. This was the greatest test of whether the height balancing was going to work. Bojangles remained sound. I was not surprised at the results, for I knew that it was going to work.

Retracing our steps to the barn, Doc was still puzzled over what he had just seen. "I can't believe that a lift could help a horse that much." I explained to him that rebalancing the body is very important to the horse's wellbeing, but the most important part of the method is teaching horseowners to become more aware of horses' physical makeup. If one wants to prevent lameness, one must be aware of a horse's conformation.

Make Horseowners Aware

As we reached the barn, I started to pull out horses at random, some of which I had never seen before. I had Doc look at their conformation for unevenness and I asked him how many

"None." of the horses he thought were even. He answered, "None." I told Doc that education was the difference, for now he could see the unevenness in a horse.

Needless to say, Jane was happy to have Bojangles moving well. Her horse was her therapy from the pressures of life, and the thought of losing Bojangles or replacing him was devastating.

Rope walking is not only a mechanical problem, it is also a physical one. Here, the rider's unawareness of the physical problems of the horse had increased the seriousness of the mechanical problems. The Bojangles case illustrates how sometimes rider, saddle and horse must be adjusted for success. Similarly there **Three** can and should be a working relationship among **Adjustments** the different professions. This can only be developed through openmindedness.

98

Chapter 9

Beau's Story

"I brought him out of pasture because he was very lame."

A.M.

No One Knew Why

On one occasion I was called by the owner of a very expensive yearling quarterhorse stud colt that had been bought as a weanling. The horse had gone lame and no one could identify the cause of the problem. I knew the owner, Tommy, and by his standards this horse was expensive. He had saved a long time to make the purchase. This colt had been kept on a mountain pasture and so the possibility existed that the colt could have fallen. We made an appointment to meet after the rest of my rounds at the little ranch-like stable where Tommy kept the colt.

Thinking about the case, I was not at all sure that there was much I could do. The colt had already been checked by the best local vet, who very rarely missed a thing. Tommy indicated Doc had suggested I should look at the colt. Perhaps there was some light I could shed.

Rodeo Practice

I arrived at the ranch in time to watch the boys roping some cattle for practice. Rodeo is a big sport in Hawaii, and I was also a roper. Tommy was on another horse out there roping the heels of a steer. When he was through, Tommy invited me to take a turn. Not wanting to refuse any practice time, I took the opportunity to rope two steers. I was a header (the guy who ropes the steer by the horns and moves the steer into position for a partner to rope the heels). This was a traditional method used by cowboys in the old days in order to brand their cattle. When we finished, we unsaddled the horses and Tommy brought out his colt Beau.

100

Beau was a small chunky guy in obvious pain. He walked out of his stall dragging his left front leg. Examination of his hoof with a hoof tester showed no sign of an abcess, or even a hint of a quittor (a very deep bruise inside the sole). To examine the tendons, I pulled Beau's leg forward as well to see if there could be a shoulder problem. There was no visible soreness. Beau did not react. However, as Tommy walked Beau away from me the horse repeatedly threw the left front leg out from his body. Again there was no outward sign like a splint or swelling.

A Dragging Left Front Leg

Beau was not going to be helped today.

Tommy indicated he had Beau on medication, but that it seemed to have no effect. He was expecting to put the colt out with his cows and hope the problem would go away. In the meantime, Beau would remain in the holding pen with the roping steers to allow him some freedom of movement.

I made arrangements to come back and observe Beau from time to time while the colt was there. This was the first time that I was actually stumped about what to do. The colt had been barefoot. There must be some reason for his lameness. What could it be? I called Doc to talk to him about the colt. We both were at a loss for answers. How do you have a lame colt that shows no reaction to testing, has never been worked, but is still lame? Enough time had passed for an abcess to break through if an

Medication Didn't Help

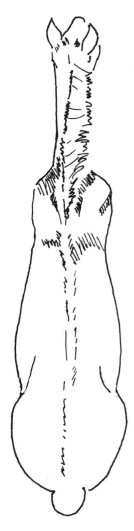

abcess were causing the lameness. Doc had even directed Tommy to soak the foot for ten days.

Then I remembered something I had forgotten to check. My mind had been absorbed with the excitement of the roping, and I was not concentrating on what I was doing. I never looked over the back, nor did I pay much attention to the angles of the colt's heels. Tommy had given me permission to check Beau any time, and there was now a reason to return. I couldn't sleep all night. I was upset with myself for not looking at the horse's back and I took my shoeing too seriously. Here was a problem that would eventually lead me to the hospital suffering from a severe tension migraine headache.

When dawn broke, I was in place at the little farm. Tommy had already fed the horses and apparently left for work. Beau was in the pen with the steers, ruling them as if it were his territory, not letting them eat any hay until he had his fill.

Behind the pen was a steep hill which was used by the family and friends of the ropers to observe the performances in the ring. This hill not only provided a good view of the arena, it offered a good view of the ocean as well. In this instance, the hill was useful for getting a top view of Beau's back. Much to my surprise, I found the answer on that hillside. Beau had a longer left leg, coupled with a curve of the neck that actually moved the hairline of his mane over to the right. The problem was a pinched nerve. This explained why he would sometimes hold the leg as if it were paralyzed. Also he would have the toe bent back underneath him, resting on the coronary band and front wall of the left front leg.

He Showed His Displeasure

I came down to examine Beau a little closer. As I stood him up, he was reluctant to put both legs together. I probed the neck and withers on the left side and he showed much displeasure by putting his ears back. Then he attempted to turn and bite me. When he knew he couldn't bite me, he tried to kick me.

Having found the problem I knew there had to be a solution.

Since Tommy wasn't around to share in the discovery, I went to the nearest store to call Doc. The vet was very receptive, but we still didn't have a solution. Eventually, placing a shoe on the right front foot to try to relieve the pressure seemed worthwhile. Next, Tommy's approval was needed. He wasn't likely to object, since the horse was lame already.

A Mentally Tired Farrier

I was so excited, I never took the time to check the heel growth of the front feet. This type of shoeing can make a farrier mentally tired. After finishing my other rounds, I went back to tell Tommy the good news. We went up on the hill so that he could see for himself. By the expression on his face, he showed it was difficult for him to believe that his horse's lameness was

103

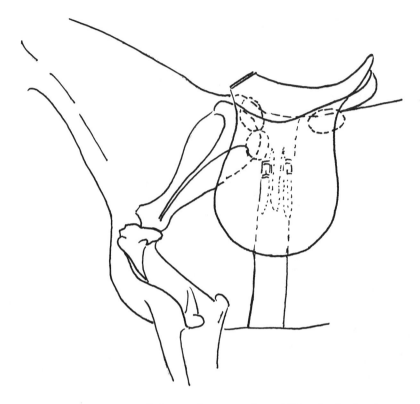

caused by a longer leg. His disbelief changed, however, when he got a closer view.

Body To The Right

We came down from the hill and Tommy brought Beau out of the pen and stood him up on the concrete. I saw something else that I did not see before. When Tommy made Beau put his front feet together, Beau's body shifted to the right. It looked as if he were going to fall over. From the rear view over the hip, it was evident that the left shoulder was more developed, and it looked rolled over to the right. Tommy walked him again, and it was clear that the left front leg was swinging to the outside while the rest of his legs were going straight. What made this more amazing was that no one saw this before.

Check His Heels

As Tommy brought Beau back to me, I examined his heels. The heel on the right was higher and the heel on the left was much lower. There was more toe growth on the left. This is commonly found with the long and short legs of an unshod horse. Tommy agreed to let me put one shoe on the colt, to see if we could reduce the pain. In fact, he said he'd try anything. I reexamined the front legs for height and estimated a difference of at least one inch and a quarter. The colt's right front leg was raised one inch. This was done by using a plastic shoe three quarters of an inch thick, nailed to a shoe a quarter of an inch thick.

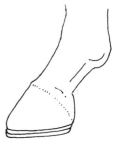

Not expecting a miracle right away, I asked Tommy if I could work the colt on the lead line and exercise him as therapy. Tommy had no objection to the method. Every day after work I monitored the progress. Beau started showing substantial improvement. The colt was led through a pace of walking over ground poles to get him to start stretching his muscles upward and forward. He was sound in two weeks with no more lameness.

Slow But Sure

I continued this process for a month and I could see the muscle development increasing evenly from side to side. In a month I reshod Beau, dropping the height of the pad an eighth inch at a time, until, eventually, Beau wore

shoes of even length on both fronts. Today he is used as a child's barrel racing horse.

The only way to explain what had happened here was to suggest that, as Beau was growing, for some reason unknown to man, his left front side grew faster than the right. This caused the right shoulder to drop lower, under the withers. When the left shoulder would be up in its correct position, the shoulder would move the spine onto the top of the right shoulder blade, pinching a nerve. By building up the muscles of the right front shoulder to match the left shoulder, I was able to readjust the position of the spine and the distance of both shoulders in relation to the spine. Here was a case of a lame horse that never had been ridden. The lameness was a fault of Beau's conformation.

Chapter 10

Topper's Story

**"I made a big mistake. I bought him
over the phone!"**

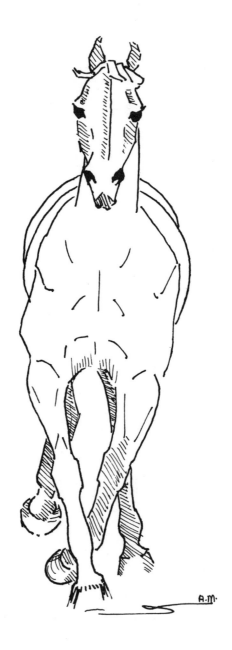

A young woman named Patty was talked into buying a horse over the phone. There are better ways to pick horses. However, this incident had a special twist.

Patty's friend, who made the sale, was concerned about Patty's recent loss of her former horse. The poor animal had become so crippled from ringbone that all walking was impossible and the horse had been put down. And a friend's friend had a great offer. The caller had just purchased two horses from a dealer in California. Eventually the friend convinced Patty to put her money on one of the pair.

Patty committed her money for the horse and couldn't back out of the deal. What next came over my phone was a horseowner's nightmare. Apparently Patty's friend also had not seen the horses. Actually, they both bought names. Patty's horse was called Topper.

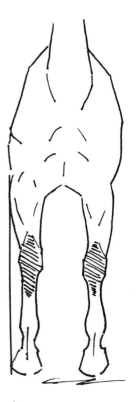

When the horses arrived by plane, and Topper came down the airplane ramp, Patty didn't know whether to laugh or cry. The horse's two front legs were severely crooked—a very bad deal for $3000. Patty admitted she really couldn't blame her friend. She really should have known better than to buy a horse without seeing it.

A Horseowner's Nightmare

I told her she was the kind of friend I would like to have.

The transaction had taken place eight

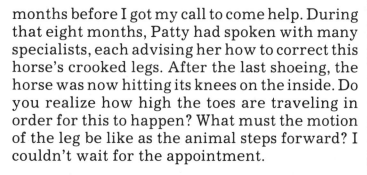

months before I got my call to come help. During
Many that eight months, Patty had spoken with many
Specialists' specialists, each advising her how to correct this
horse's crooked legs. After the last shoeing, the
Advice horse was now hitting its knees on the inside. Do
you realize how high the toes are traveling in
order for this to happen? What must the motion
of the leg be like as the animal steps forward? I
couldn't wait for the appointment.

What would be the width of the chest?
How would the hooves leave the ground? How
would a hoof land on the ground? What would be
the swinging motion of the leg? How would the
knee be opening and closing? These were the
questions running through my mind as I started
to prepare myself for what I was going to
encounter. It was hard not to be a little anxious
to see what a $3000 mistake looked like. I brought
my 8mm movie camera that I use to take movies
of cases I would like to study further. Viewing
the horse through the camera lens helps cut out
all background objects that can distort your
vision. It also allows the observer to focus on a
particular area without worrying about distractions.

The farm had an old dairy which had been
Study transformed into stables. The principal feature
Movies was a long concrete aisle that led down to several
barns and pastures. This was actually paradise
for horses. The pastures were very hilly, which
gave the horses a lot of exercise even if they
weren't ridden much at all. Patty took me to
Topper's stall. She was right. Buying this horse

110

was a mistake. The horse had both front legs turning outward very badly. Topper was a big horse, about 16.2 hands. He had unusually long cannon bones, probably the longest I have ever seen. Patty walked Topper toward me and away from me, while I filmed his motion with my camera. The horse's movement was fascinating to watch.

One Went East, One Went West

Patty said she had used several experienced horseshoers who worked with this kind of problem, but they had not gotten the horse to walk without interfering. When she told me this, I was really on the spot. It was interesting to find out that every one of them had prepared the hoof the same way. They all cut the outside of the hoof lower than the inside of the hoof on both front legs. As I watched Topper through the camera, I saw something that apparently everyone else had missed. Topper was landing on the outside of his foot first, then rotating inward with his legs. Finally he ended up landing on the inside of his foot. Topper's right front leg was worse than his left.

When Topper turned around to walk away, the abnormalities of his knee motion, the real cause of his movement problem became clear. His knees opened up, going to the outside of the body, then closed to the inside of the body. This forced the foot to swing in then out, thus allowing the toe of each foot to come in contact with a fetlock or knee joint. Topper was very narrow at the chest, so this helped to limit how much

Outward Opening Knees

111

**Front
Problem
Compensation**

stretch he would have as he threw his legs out to the side.

The hind legs were shortening in stride and twisting at the hocks to help breakover. This was in compensation for the front problems. This horse could frustrate any horseshoer. I kept the camera rolling, constantly observing how each foot was traveling as it hit the ground. Then, as the horse walked away from me, I concentrated on the swing of the legs. This was the best view to see the outer body line and see where the legs moved to help the horse keep its balance. I discovered that his front end was moving toward the right and the hind end was tracking toward the left. Any consideration of riding stopped for Patty when she revealed her overall concern about Topper getting tangled up with his front legs and falling down. The last horseshoer had just given up, she said. He felt that he had tried everything that he could.

In fact, the last farrier had tried everything I would have tried. He had fitted rolled toe shoes, half round shoes, and a round memphis bar on the shoes.

The memphis is especially interesting. This is a small bar mounted on top of the ground surface of the shoe. It is usually a round bar stock no wider than three sixteenths of an inch, which is normally applied in the middle of the shoe, straight or slanted to whichever side the farrier wants the hoof to break over. In Topper's case the bar was placed toward the inside of the shoe.

Each previous analysis of the horse's movement had failed because the knee factor was neglected. All frontal movement was a direct result of the knee motion.

The motion impediment started at the knee, but because of the treatment the right front now had the whole leg turned toward the outside. The previous methods of shoeing had actually interfered with the motion of the joints. The animal had to forcibly walk in the strange manner that was described above in order to reduce pain. This horse was a mess.

Up to this point, all that had ever been written for horseshoeing were how to books. If there were any textbooks which explained principles, I never found them. So when it came to the movement of joints, all farriers were babes in the woods. Anything that happened to the knees or above was new territory. Only occasionally would an individual horseshoer look above the knee to consider the horse's full leg movement. The standard procedure was to watch how the foot landed on the ground and nothing more.

The problems with Topper's motion had nothing to do with the shoes that were used. They should have worked. They didn't work because of the way the hoof was cut.

113

Splay Footedness

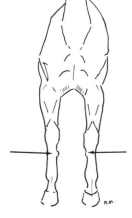

All horseshoers know that for a horse having splay footedness (turning out), the appropriate response is to lower the outside wall. In this instance, the approved procedure actually was an aggravation. The knee was designed to move toward the outside of the body. The unusual design motion may have given the horse greater balance to compensate for Topper's pronounced narrowness, but there is no way to be certain without further research. Cutting the outside of the hoof wall, and lifting the inside of the hoof wall, stopped the knee from being able to close correctly. This, in turn, also interfered with the fetlock's ability to close naturally as well. So pressure of the joints was now transferred to the middle of the joints.

In Goes The Elbow Joint

This pressure made Topper twist his front legs further toward the outside. This motion included rotating the inside of the knee joint, while rotating the inside of the fetlock joint further in toward the opposite side. This peculiar motion occurred because there was no developed chest muscles to prevent the twisting of the leg. The point of the shoulder would turn to the outside and the elbow joint would collapse in toward the body. It was this stance that created the splints on both front legs. Meanwhile, cutting the outside of the hoof wall made the swing of the leg worse, because the animal then had to lead off with its toe swinging inward to gain the momentum that it needed in order to accomplish the twist to allow the knee joint to close. Admittedly, this description sounds confusing and impossible, but it's true.

Obviously the solution was to do the opposite of what everyone had been trying to do. Stop trying to correct the leg, raise the outside back up, and basically leave everything to work the way this body had been designed to work. Confirmation for this strategy came when I learned from Patty that she had never had this problem when she first got the animal. These problems arose after everyone talked her into having corrections made to Topper. She said he actually was doing fine at the start.

So Do The Opposite

When I got there, Topper had on a half round shoe. But the outside wall was much lower than the inside wall. This was partially due to a shim insert put in on the inside to increase the height. Topper's natural movement was to break over his inside toe, which allowed the knee to close in its proper position. The only way this could be accomplished now would be to force the leg with a higher swing in and then out, causing the toe to lead the swing and hitting the knee or fetlock joints from in back of the front legs.

It looked like the arc was the main problem that should be dealt with first. I knew that making any drastic changes on a sore horse could easily make the problem worse on the other extreme. I took Topper's shoes off and examined his stance again, closely observing the outline of his front legs starting from the outside of the shoulder all the way down to the hoof. The knee position actually was inside the outer body line. The leg looked like a warped fence board,

First, The Arc

115

Provide Free Breakover

bowing in. The outside wall was flaring out drastically. Until now, no one had addressed this as a possible problem. Topper's motion without the shoes was better.

The shoeing solution to this problem goes against all correction principles. Put it back the way it was. If it isn't broken, don't fix it. I raised the outside wall a little, keeping it about three eighths of an inch longer on the outside. Then I formed my shoe so that it was shaped more like a ring on the inside. The outside was tapered narrower, like a back shoe. A half round was wedged at the toe, back to the first nail hole on the outside to the second nail hole on the inside, having the ends flat. This insured that Topper would have free breakover on the inside portion of the hoof, where he needed it. Also, the tapering of the outside wall allowed some of the outside wall to be removed, so there would not be any wall pressure that could force the leg to turn. By doing this, I was trying to work on reducing the inward arc of the flight of the leg.

Reduce The Arc

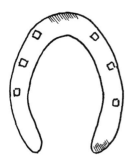

Patty had realized that no one was ever going to change the front legs, but there was reason to hope that, if the hoof could be made to appear straight without actually turning the leg, then it wouldn't be as noticeable. My hunch was right. Cosmetically the hoof looked almost straight. These corrections actually reduced the arc of the inward swing between the fetlock joint and the hoof. The motion changed that much immediately.

As we worked on this procedure time after time, Topper began walking straighter. He never really gave up the swing of the knee. However, we were able to get the leg to move forward, and land each hind foot in the hoof prints of the front. **A Straighter Walk**

This was one of the rare cases helped by being left alone. Returning him to a more natural state allowed the horse to stop tripping and stay sound. Now I ask everyone who wants me to correct a leg problem like this if the correction is to improve the horse's motion, or is the correction merely to please the eye? This horse went on to win its points to be considered for a permanent championship card. The judges, although they saw the leg going out, couldn't fault the horse when he was tracking straight one foot behind the other. Topper won many pleasure classes as well.

This was a good case in which cutting the foot in the wrong place was the real problem. I call this case the exception to the exception. **The Real Problem**

Dear Mr. Gonzales,

     As a fellow blacksmith, I am very interested in your articles on Balancing the Horse. If you have any of this information available to the public, I would appreciate it if you would inform me as to what is available.

                Yours Truly,
                Wm. E.
                MacMillan

Chapter 11

Balance The Rider

How do you balance the horse for the rider's weight?

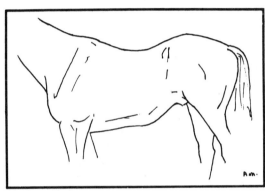

16. Sway Back

Once a horse has had a rider on its back, the horse no longer maintains its own balance. The horse now has to adjust its movement and stance in order to accommodate the rider's weight. When a horse moves forward, or makes turns, it produces forward momentum. Then when one adds the extra weight of a rider, the new, increased momentum can throw the horse off balance. A horse's physical development, particularly in the hooves, changes substantially with the increased stress caused by the rider's weight. The adjusted motion, with horse and rider, reflects pressures on the skeletal structure as well as the muscle structure. Upper body

19. Sickle Hock

The Adjustment Period

Education Needed

pressures now influence the lower leg pressures. Lower leg pressures will show up in hoof wear.

Most people don't realize that when a horse is being trained to take a rider, the horse takes a while to adjust to the changes. During this adjustment period, problems can occur in the form of lower leg disorders. In many cases, horses will have unusual swelling in the fetlock. Forging is a big problem—this is where the horse takes its hind feet and hits its front feet at either the toe of the shoe or heel of the shoe or foot. Interference of the legs, where the front or hind legs hit each other at the ankles, and even stumbling are common problems.

In the past it has been suggested that all these problems are related to shoeing. This can be true, but not for the reason that many people believe. Shoeing, in many cases, is not the cause but the solution. These problems arise from the balance adjustments the horse is undergoing. Admittedly, there is some incompetence in the horse world. Actually, a better word would be naivete. There are horseshoers in the profession who are not competent. This problem would not be so bad if someone had taken the time to educate these people. This is not a proposal for a professional school, or for setting up standard tests for horseshoers to pass. Instead, someone should set up research to test whatever theories are suggested or promoted. In this way, the horse world could be educated by reading the published results. If people would press for research in horseshoeing performed by horse-shoers, incompetence would drop off rapidly.

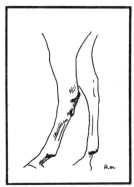

20. Curb

For some reason, certain of the apparently naive or incompetent horseshoers have a thriving business. Also, sometimes even the evidently competent horseshoers make the same mistakes that the naive horseshoers make. Every horseshoer believes that what he is doing is right for the horse. Often he is right and produces sound horses, which is the bottom line.

The arguments about who's right and who's wrong seem almost endless, and trying to choose between them has been like beating my head against a brick wall. The wall won't move, but one will accomplish one thing—getting a headache. When I became interested in one legged lameness, I realized that the occurrence of this problem with horses was related to the quality of the riding standards. The goal for many riders became perfect execution of performance. No one can be blamed for wanting that. But the horse's problems arose when people began setting standards of performance for their horses that the horses were physically unable to achieve in a consistent fashion. This caused the eventual breakdown of the animal. One legged lameness is a direct result of the long leg and short leg problem.

New Standards, New Problems

Over the last 15 years, the philosophy of riding has changed. The quest to win at all costs became more evident. Monetary returns overruled lasting soundness. Desperation because of

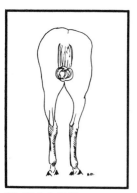

21. High Left Hip

financial burdens stretched horses' strength, patience, and endurance to the limits. When I was a teenager, I knew that horses were broken to ride when they were three years old. Then, they were rested over the winter and brought back as four-year-olds and finished off. This gave the animal's body time to mature and have its bone structure fully set.

Today, horses are being broken as young as one and a half years old, then are brought back as two-year-olds and, in many cases, expected to be perfect performance horses. By this time they are three and one half years of age. In this society, we have set the standard that the return value of a horse is at its peak before the animal reaches the age of seven years old. For many horseowners this has become a burden, because the number of horses reaching the ridden age of seven years old that have remained sound and free from any leg problems is really small. In this I am only including horses that have made it in today's society to the age of seven free from drugs. Some people say that horses can't make it that long without some kind of help because of the rigorous show schedules. Meanwhile, the horses are the ones that really suffer.

The Seven Year Limit

Most of the lame horses that I have worked on were horses that were ridden. There were very few cases of young horses going lame, except for an abcess in the foot, or an injury. The majority of lame horses acquired their problems after they were ridden. Some people will say that the lameness did not show up until the shoes were put on. In many cases I agree. However, when I question the horseowners about how much riding was done after the shoes were put on, the answer is usually double. The shoes allow the horseowner a clear conscience to ride harder, because the horse's feet are protected against getting sore.

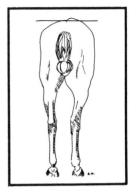

22. High Right Hip

As the horse carries a rider, it will have to move its legs beyond the position that it would stride alone. When a rider's weight is on the horse's back, there is added pressure on the rib cage and spine of the horse. If the saddle position is right, one will not have any pressure on the vertebrae of the back or the withers. The pressure should be on the rib cage. Now if the saddle is set too far forward on the withers of the horse, then one will have both vertebrae pressure and shoulder blade pressure. This is very important to note. Remember, the chest cavity is connected to the shoulder by muscle alone. This muscle allows the chest cavity to go up and down, which would offer some relief from pressure to the vertebrae of the withers, but the big problem is pressure on the shoulder blades. As the chest cavity moves up and down, it also moves the rider closer, and in some cases, on top of the shoulder blades. Such motion can cause the horse to drop its leg to the ground sooner than it would if there were no weight on its back. This explains problems that can arise when people buy nice movers that they have seen moving freely on the lead line without a rider. After three or four riding sessions, the buyer

It's Only Muscle

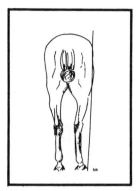

23. Hind Side Balance

can't figure out why the horse is now a bad mover.

Since forward saddle position can interfere with frontal motion, this interference with the motion will combine with the drop effect of the horse as it shortens its stride. This drop effect moves the head of the horse back to the hands of the rider, creating more forward momentum shift of the rider. The rider will now end up atop the horse's frontal weight, bringing about what is known as riding heavy in the forehand. Most riders are not aware of what happens next. As the riders try to hold this horse up, their balance has now shifted to their shoulders, pulling back. Then the pressure is pushed downward towards the toes of their feet. This thrusts most of their weight onto the shoulder of the horse. It is important not only to observe the horse's movement, with the rider upon its back, but also to analyze the rider's positions as well.

How does this forward balance affect the hind end? It forces the hind end to move behind the horse, making it impossible for the horse to step under itself without sending the rider straight out of the saddle. Many times I have been able to correct a horse problem just by adjusting a saddle, commenting on rider position, and making people aware of how riding can interfere with a horse's movement.

Rider Interference

With experience at riding and training in my youth, I had an edge in understanding what was going on with riding and training. This

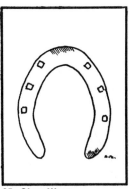

25. Shoe Wear

experience also helps me understand how riding and shoeing can work together or against one another. I have worked with and observed all different types of horses and riding. I have worked on almost every type of breed, and they all have motion lameness in common. There is, however, a pattern relating the rider position and lameness. More than the rider position is involved, for there are always circumstances influencing the findings, circumstances that have contributed to the lameness. A lame horse can be healed or crippled by the type of riding, the type of training programs, and the type of horseshoeing.

Influences, Not Causes

These are called circumstances, because, while they do not cause the lameness, they do influence it. Lameness is caused by the short leg and long leg problem. Later I will discuss the position of the rider on the back and how it affects lameness. First, understand that there are exceptions to every rule. But this is not the place to discuss how and why they exist.

Navicular

The short front leg will consistently suffer from tendon problems (high and low bows), suspensory and ligament problems, and rear pressure-related navicular. The long front leg will consistently show ringbone, sidebone, knee problems, splints, and a new discovery of mine (frontal pressure-related navicular), and shoulder problems.

The hind legs have fewer problems than the front, but the problems are just as severe.

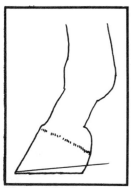

26. Lower Heel

The short hind leg will consistently display hock problems (particularly spavin problems), and upper hip soreness. The long hind leg will suffer regularly from stifle problems, tendon problems, and gluteal muscle pulls (this is the upper hip muscle). Six years of study and experience have gone into identifying the causes of these diseases.

How does rider position affect these problems? Tendon and ligament problems occur when there is an overstretching of the leg. This overstretching can be caused by the horse, by slipping, or stepping into a hole, or even by pulling off a shoe. When the problems result from riding, in many cases they occur because a rider shifts his weight onto the side that is affected. When the foot starts to leave the ground, the sudden shift forward by the rider forces the leg to overextend for balance. This causes tissue to tear.

Tearing Tissue

Rear pressure-related navicular refers to the tendon pressing against the navicular bone. The riding position which would aggravate this condition consists of regularly falling off balance to the vulnerable side of the horse. The poor balance of the rider is partly due to the lowness of the shoulder blade. It lacks the muscle development to support the saddle.

Poor Rider Balance

Longer front leg problems, including ringbone, sidebone, and knee problems, are basic concussive problems. This is a result of shorter or higher motion of the front legs. Ringbone and sidebone and some knee problems are a result of lower leg motion, along with stride retardation. If the horse is unable to move its leg from the shoulder because of shoulder constriction by the rider, then the horse will be forced to use more fetlock and knee action in order to move its leg forward. This upward arc leads the horse to look like it is covering a lot of ground when it is actually making small strides. The foot contacts the ground right underneath the rider's position in order to carry the rider's weight.

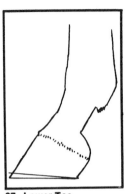

27. Lower Toe

Knee Problems

Some knee problems result from the foot contacting the ground first at the toe. The toe strikes the ground first, then the heel follows. This leads to the fetlock closing first, then the knee joint follows. Variations on how far back the knee will have to close and where the rider's weight may be at the time determine whether the animal fractures the knee or gets arthritis. The rider's position may be too far forward on the horse's withers, interfering with the freedom of the back and downward swing of the shoulder blade. An inside splint can be found on a horse with an overdeveloped shoulder at the top of the shoulder blade. This overdeveloped shoulder forces the animal to step outside of its body line in order to even the shoulders. Outward swing in the stride drops the shoulder blade back and inward. This causes a rider to be thrust upon the overdeveloped shoulder. This constant contact creates soreness, so the horse can only protect itself by throwing its leg outward. These horses will have wide chests.

Overdeveloped Shoulder

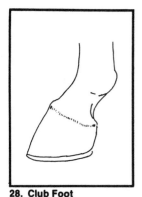

28. Club Foot

Outside splints occur because of outside pressure of the leg. The corresponding motion would be a leg walking inward, towards the center of the horse. This stride inward allows the shoulder blade to move outward and down. The foot will rotate forward, rolling to the outside of the hoof, thus forcing pressure to the outside of the leg. The chest on these horses is narrow.

My Current Theory

My current navicular theory points to frontal pressure coming down from the coronary band in front of the hoof. This pressure pushes back and down on the coffin and short pastern joint, which puts pressure on the navicular bone from that angle. This is displayed by the toe hitting the ground first following by contact by the heel. I feel that this joint actually over closes first, then the fetlock closes, and so on. Overriding the withers aggravates this problem.

Rider Shifts

Shoulder problems could be a result of the rider getting out of position. Shifting by the rider can cause a pinch, muscle tears or muscle damage. The rider's imbalance could be caused by a poorly fitting saddle or even by the wrong equipment being used, such as a breast collar to hold the saddle forward.

What are the causes of short leg problems? Hock problems are generally the result of shortness of stride. Since the leg does not have to travel as high, the animal will barely raise its toe off the ground. This means the horse is overworking its fetlock joint and barely exercising the hock joint. The hock becomes stiff from taking the jarring action of the drag. Then the hock will have to rotate outward in order to maintain breakover. This outward rotation leads to spavin problems. Stiff hocks can also cause upper hip soreness, which usually arises from compensation. When the hocks become sore, the horse will want to stand on its toe and relieve the pressure to the hocks. A horseshoer can read this soreness by feeling the stiffness in the leg when it is picked up. There will be redness at the white line, mainly at the toe. The horse will start to stand with its legs going out behind itself, creating a forward tilt to the hips to relieve pressure.

30. Rider Position

The long hind leg usually has more frequent problems. This is the leg where the stifle would be affected first. Stifle problems arise from the inward swing of the leg in order to level the hips. Remember, the longer hind leg will go up first, and then down to level. The downward motion is a result of the inward swing. It is the only way that the leg can move to level the hips for balance. When the leg moves in, it places more pressure on the stifle joint. A young horse, or an older horse out to pasture that has been allowed to graze its life away, can have stifle problems. Obviously conformation can cause the problem.

Stifle

Young Or Old

What about the horse that does not have the typical build? Stifle problems in young horses that have never been ridden, and many older horses which have been ridden, are caused by the stomach. When the stomach enlarges due

129

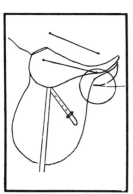

31. Saddle Pressure

to weight, the back muscle loses its strength and the stomach muscles take over. Gravitational pull obliges the horse to step under or step outside of its body, thus putting more strain on the stifle area. The weight of the stomach will also pull the hips forward, which puts more stress on the stifle joint as well.

Tendon problems and gluteal muscle pulls are a result of the leg going in toward the center of the body. This inward stride causes the leg to stretch forward more than it should.

How does the rider influence this? The longer hind leg has a tendency to throw riders forward when it reaches break over point, that is, when the foot is nearly ready to leave the ground. This forward thrust will unseat a rider, and the rider's reaction will be to resist it. Now if a rider stays in place, then the stress is not bad. If the rider is thrown off balance, then the rider's **Regaining** reaction is to regain riding position. Regaining **Rider** this position is sometimes attempted by a back- **Rider** ward push toward the hip that unseated the per- **Position** son in the first place. Usually, the rider will regain the position when the leg is under the body. The damage is done when the rider forces the body weight back into the saddle, adding weight which catches the stifle in a closed position. This added weight causes an increasing amount of pressure on the joint.

~~

This is only the beginning of the awareness

130

ness process. There are many more questions that need to be answered. I have just given you the tip of the iceberg. I ask you to question and digest what I have told you and prepare yourselves for more education. My ideas are just one set of many, but what is important is that answers are coming. I have had confirmation from three research veterinarians that what I am doing with my theory has validity. The response in the shoeing community has been great and horseowners are now more aware. Working together is what it's all about.

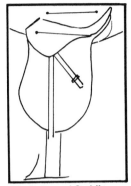

32. Balanced Saddle

The United States Pony Clubs, Inc.

Dear Tony,

As you are no doubt aware, your contribution to the USPC Annual Meeting was extremely well received. The demand for repeat performances will attest to that. I did want to thank you very much for all your efforts. This was the first time we have had anything on corrective shoeing and, obviously, the first time anyone has approached shoeing from the top down.

Again, thanks for providing something new and interesting for our many volunteers.

Sincerely yours,
George L. Helwig
Executive Director

Chapter 12

Justice's Story

"I now need your help!"

"I Need Your Help."

Occasionally, it is a great pleasure to be able to say "I told you so."

One morning as I shoed horses at a familiar barn I encountered a young woman named Valerie, just back from a horse show. Leaving her truck, she hurried over to where I was shoeing. I was busy making a shoe for a horse that I was working on, when my train of thought was broken by this young lady.

"My Horse Is Lame."

"Tony, I need your help. My horse is lame." This was a fairly familiar start to a working relationship. Looking up from my task, I noticed a very pretty face with a desperate expression. I told her I would look at her horse after I had finished my obligation to shoe the horse I was shoeing. She agreed to wait.

An Immobile Leg

Actually she had no choice. As I wrapped up my work, I knew I was setting myself up for further criticism. Lounging by the barn was a man who did not like what I was doing. He was especially insistent that everyone come to him first. Since there was no real chance of exercising diplomacy here, I had to be very certain of what I was going to say. Otherwise I could get into trouble. As Val led Justice out of the stall, I observed that the animal could barely get its left front foot over the little board guard in front of the stall doorway. This is a serious sign, proving that the horse is having problems lifting the leg.

All it takes is a little simple deductive reasoning.

134

Now Val owned a very expensive horse and she came from an affluent family. Having one of the best horses in the area go lame on her was devastating for Val.

A Very Expensive Horse

I asked her what happened.

The trouble began at a show, maneuvering the horse in a couple of jumping classes. After one of the jumps, the horse started to go lame. Several people at the show examined the horse for her, they all thought that the horse might have a bruise. This was a reasonable conclusion. However, I could not agree with it. When she led the horse down the aisle, the horse's sore hoof was hitting the ground with a normal impact—that is not characteristic of a bruise. I asked her if he seemed to be stiff that morning when she took him out of the stall, but he hadn't been.

"How was he when you got to the show, and took him off the trailer? Was he stiff then?"

"No." She continued, "His warm up was great, he felt good. The first two classes he won—the flat classes." A flat class is a class in which the horse or rider will be judged going around the ring, at a walk, trot, and canter. No jumping.

Jumping To Lameness

The next question was the critical one. "What happened when you went into the fence—the one where you first noticed him go off?"

"Well," she said, "we both got into the

The Wrong Angle

fence wrong. Actually, I tried to take it at the wrong angle and he had to make a last minute adjustment. But he went over just beautifully."

Next question: was the ring rocky? "No, it was all grass."

A Shoulder Problem

My reason for concluding that the real problem was in the shoulder and that he may have simply twisted it, started with an awareness that the weather had brought drought conditions to many areas. The ground was very hard, like concrete. "Were you unseated in the jump?"

"Yes."

"Were you going in to the left?"

"Yes."

I picked up the left front leg and stretched it forward. Justice reacted strongly. Turning to Val, I said "I believe that your horse has a shoulder problem."

"But how could this be?"

"With the limited knowledge I have, I feel that when you got into the fence wrong, the horse probably had to compensate for the angle at which you took off. So, what happened was that he had to stick the left front leg out in a way that exposed his shoulder blade. Then when you came out of the saddle towards the left, the added weight probably forced a strained muscle."

She looked at me with a very puzzled face. I knew what kind of reaction I was going to get, because the same thing had once happened to me while riding a horse. One could almost watch the thoughts running through Val's head, "He is saying I caused that. Ha! I'm a good rider. This guy's off his rocker."

With her eyes screaming disbelief. I told her that she should get other opinions as well. It wasn't likely that I would ever hear from her again, but I had an obligation to tell her my

Don't Stretch My Leg!

An Exposed Shoulder Blade

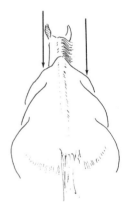

Disbelieving Eyes

"I Told You So."

conclusion. Perhaps my greatest problem as a horseshoer was that I took my work too seriously. There is no point in saying anything unless you are certain that you know what you are talking about.

It was easy to feel a little sorry for Val, but there was also a relief. If I was right, I was about to be placed in a very difficult situation. I'd have to come up with an answer. Shoulders were a field I was just starting to study. At that time, most of my therapy with sore shoulders consisted of treatment with linament rubs. There was no reason to believe that shoeing would help.

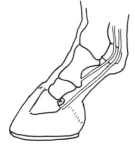

If Val did not get back in touch within a week, it was unlikely that I would hear from her at all. She didn't call. As time passed, I totally forgot about Val's problem. Who would have guessed that three months after I had given her my opinion, she would give me the chance to say "I told you so."

I Thought The Horse Was Fine

Three months had passed when I stopped at my usual feed store to pick up some grain for my horses. While I was loading the pickup, a Porsche drove up. Val crossed over to me with news that she was going to be back in touch with me. I was quite surprised.

All this time I thought that the horse was fine. It was easy to believe that my first opinion had been wrong.

Evidently, however, I had been right. Val explained, "My horse is still lame. We have tried everything. We thought he might have navicular. We tried several different types of shoe, but he's still lame, and he's now on medication."

My Horse Is Still Lame

I hesitated a few minutes not wanting to show any signs of eagerness, but I was psyched. Here was a great chance to find out if my shoeing technique would work on a shoulder problem.

Val admitted to me that, after all which had done, it looked like the horse was suffering from a shoulder problem. I was not surprised that they couldn't find the problem lower in the leg. The horse's stance would indicate if there were navicular involvement. It was pleasing to have experts agree with my conclusion, but I was not ready to help her yet.

If I worked on this horse, without an understanding that there would be no outside interference, Val could change her mind before I got a fair chance to try the shoeing technique. So, before I agreed to help her, I clarified that I would not try anything until she promised I could work on the horse without any interference.

Horseshoeing Can Be Heartbreaking

Horseshoeing can be heartbreaking. Just on the edge of a breakthrough, an owner will hear criticism and lose his nerve. If the owner doesn't understand the farrier's aim, criticism

A Return To Old Methods

of the new technique will panic him. Then the owner changes the shoes.

In some cases I have treated lame horses and made them sound only to have owners buckle under criticism and return to the old methods which had failed to help. Then, tragically, in many cases, the horses again went lame.

I told Val that we could meet the next afternoon at 5:30. The previous shoer was available to discuss his work with me. I called him.

It is always better to find out what has already been done. Otherwise, one might be putting the horse through the inconvenience of starting over, prolonging the pain.

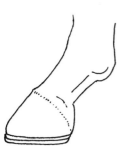

Using The Plastic Shoe

Jim was pleasant over the phone. In fact, he had heard about something I was doing and that I was getting good results. I thanked him for the kind words and asked him what he had already done. Jim admitted that he was baffled. At first he had tried an egg butt bar, with pads and silicone, without results. Then he went to a plastic shoe, eliminating all metal and weight to the foot, so there would be less shock on the hoof as it struck the ground. I liked the man's thinking, and agreed with his decisions. Jim told me that he was using the plastic shoe on the horse now. It would be impractical for him to meet me the next afternoon, so I told him Val would report my findings.

It was nice to find a colleague interested in

letting me look at one of his horses without feeling threatened. Val was a little late meeting me at the barn, but it didn't matter.

The horse had been moved from the barn where I had met her the first time. The new stable was like paradise. The arena was a fenced in polo field, and the view was spectacular with high mountains in the background and a striking view of the ocean. Remembering I was not being paid to sightsee, I pulled my hoof testers from the truck.

It was immediately obvious the horse was sore on the left front leg, because the horse was pointing the leg forward, keeping very little weight on it. When a horse does this, assume there is a bruise in the foot. When the horse has its foot in the air forward, the stance indicates the horse is sore in the heel or in the back half of the hoof. However, a horse will also do this with a tendon pull, bruises at the sesamoids—located at the back of the fetlock—as well as the dreaded condition, navicular.

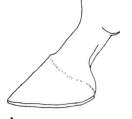

Many things suggest causes for lameness in a horse like Val's and each cause suggests a range of treatments. The real problem is deciding which line of thought to try first.

This time I started with the foot. Applying hoof testers to the sole, I began squeezing to find the one part of the sole that the horse might have bruised stepping on a rock. Nothing, no flinching. Then I tested the frog. I placed pressure on

Look From The Knee Down

the center of the frog, to see if navicular involvement was responsible. Then I pulled the frog from side to side. This would expose any hidden bruises. Again, no response.

Now came the tricky part.

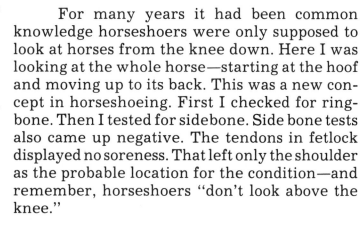

For many years it had been common knowledge horseshoers were only supposed to look at horses from the knee down. Here I was looking at the whole horse—starting at the hoof and moving up to its back. This was a new concept in horseshoeing. First I checked for ringbone. Then I tested for sidebone. Side bone tests also came up negative. The tendons in fetlock displayed no soreness. That left only the shoulder as the probable location for the condition—and remember, horseshoers "don't look above the knee."

Standing back from the horse I assessed the overall conformation. Justice was well formed, no fault there. I then stepped onto a chair and stood behind the horse to look at his shoulders from a rear view.

Varied Muscle Development

What I saw did not surprise me at this point. It was becoming commonplace for me to see varied muscle development as well as shoulder length differences on most horses. At this point I became more rider oriented. Since I have ridden horses, and also trained a few, I know how people ride. It was time to question Val, because it was obvious there was something she was not telling me.

142

Val had brought Justice out. He was beautiful—almost black, standing 16.2 hands and had a very gentle presence. This was proper breeding. Nonetheless I was sad to see Justice come from his stall heavily favoring his left front leg. For the first time, I observed the left shoulder was higher than the right. He was attractively even at the hips, though he was starting to lose his muscle tone. Justice didn't look like the same horse I first examined three months earlier. It was amazing how much muscle a horse loses when he just stands around.

A Higher Left Shoulder

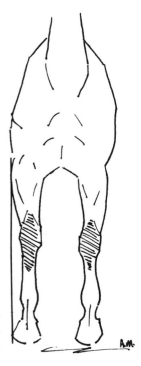

There were many questions to ask Val. Eventually, I worked up to the most important one. "Does he ever leave his stall?"

"Very little. I was told to leave him in. If I take him out it is for very short walks."

Scanning his feet, I noticed the plastic shoes. They were about three quarters of an inch thick on both front feet. At this point the train of thought becomes tricky. I knew that I would need to build the right hind to level Justice. However, rather than go through all the trouble of padding the right hind, what if I just removed the left front plastic shoe. A replacement with a training plate would be sufficiently thin. Of course, the left front foot must remain protected.

I fastened the training plate on to the left front. Val went off to get her long lead line. I wanted to see the horse move. There was no

Too Optimistic?

reason to expect any miracle right away, but I had a hunch the solution to this problem would be a simple one. A simple solution, in fact, that might have been overlooked.

Growing Doubts

As Justice paraded down the hill, he was limping, there was no change. When we reached the ring I asked her to walk him to the right. Now there was a noticeable limping. It appeared that my hope was, perhaps, too optimistic. I then asked her to trot the animal to the right. Again, there was no change, the horse was still off. Next Val led the horse in the opposite direction. The change of direction also made no difference in Justice's lameness. My doubts were growing stronger. Val's face was starting to show signs of major disappointment.

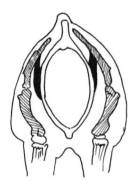

Staying confident was turning into a challenge. I had been so certain that this would work that now I was beginning to feel like a fool. How could I be so bold as to think that I could come up with an answer that no one else suggested?

Something Popped Free

It was time to pull out all the stops. I instructed Val to make Justice canter. I knew that he was hurting but I still believed my hunch was correct about the shoulder injury and what was causing it. Justice was reluctant at first. He had tried to run faster at a trot, and this was not an easy movement for him. He sort of lurched up his front end. Two strides later something happened in his left front shoulder as if something had popped free. Justice was sound.

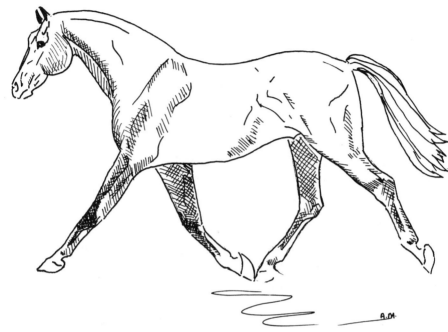

Val and I stood there frozen with our mouths open unable to believe our eyes.

"Pinch me, Val."

"Pinch me, Val, I must be dreaming." But this was no time for dramatics. We had to be certain he was sound. Val stopped Justice and made him reverse direction. He was just as sound going to the right. Curiously enough, I was puzzled. What was the explanation of what had happened?

Feeling Good Again

Justice was feeling good, starting to buck and kick out as if he were a colt again. One could see in this horse's eyes that he was suddenly free from pain.

Writing this down, some of these cases can

Analyzing The Results

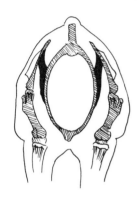

sound far fetched, but every one is true. After analyzing the results, I had confirmed my hunch.

This is how I reached my conclusion on the first day. When Val initially came into the barn to ask my help, I had assumed that she was in competition with another rider, perhaps as rider of the year or horse of the year. This suggested that sometimes a miscalculation occurred because of the quest to win. Perhaps Val had gotten into the fence wrong and then had forced Justice to extend his shoulder blade. In my mind I could picture Val becoming unseated and landing on the exposed shoulder. Possibly she had pulled the shoulder blade away from the muscles attached to the spine.

When I removed the plastic shoe from the left front foot, I allowed the muscles to relax. Then the canter encouraged the stretching of the hurt muscle, or the constricted muscle that was causing pain. Val brought the horse down to a walk. This took some time before she succeeded. Justice was feeling extremely good. It was no time to let him overdo his workout. The way he was acting, there was some danger he might accidentally pull something else.

Allowing The Muscle To Stretch

Val and I were both in a state of disbelief as we walked Justice back to the barn up the hill. All signs of his limping were gone. It was unusual for me to see such immediate results. I had never seen a horse go sound that fast. They often improve after a few days—but never immediately. In some of my cases, I would have to

146

return two or three times within two weeks just to find the correct height to make the horse right.

Now I do not advocate this method as the best or only cure. Even so, this can be an extra tool for the shoeing box, or the edge for the horse-owner to identify what could be wrong with the animal.

I left Val on a positive note. "Remember to call me if there are any further problems. I want to see the horse in a week, if he stays sound. Take it easy with the exercise and no jumping." Val agreed.

Three days later I was shoeing a horse at another barn when a young man came running up to me in a very excited state. He called out, "What did you do to the horse? How did you shoe it?"

I was startled by his excitement. More importantly, I did not know what he was talking about. Perhaps he was just interested in learning how a shoe was put on a horse. I then proceeded to tell him how it was done. When he stopped me I realized that he wanted something different. After an apology for his excitement, the young man introduced himself.

John was a visiting vet student from a university in Colorado, working with one of the local veterinarians in the area. Few people are so sincere and intense. He went on, "I just saw a

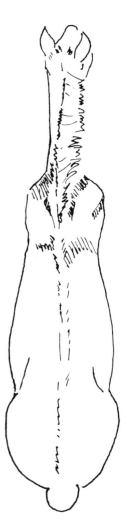

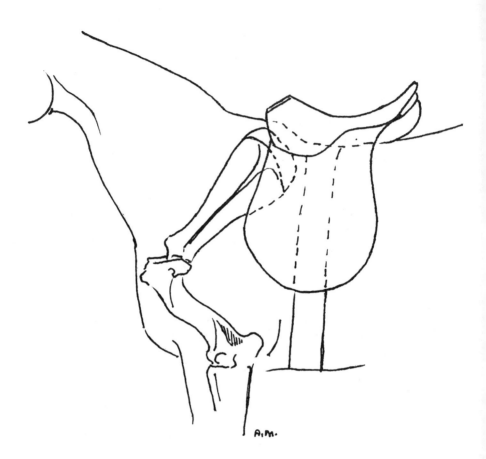

A,M.

A New Shoeing Technique girl whose horse you worked on three days ago. She told us what you had done to her horse. The last time I saw the horse it was lame. Today it's sound. What did you do? What kind of special shoe did you use?"

The freshman vet was asking me so many questions that I had to interrupt him to explain that I didn't have a special shoe. Instead, I was working on a new shoeing technique as well as a

148

different philosophy. He was eager to have me explain. As a start, I admitted to him that my results were still in the experimental stage. There was a lot to learn yet from the results of my work. He had to know where I got the ideas for a new philosophy. John's face was a study in itself as I began my story. The theory started to form in my mind with a question. Why do horses go lame in one foot rather than two feet at the same time? In my heart I knew there would be no peace for Tony Gonzales until someone answered that question.

Why Lame In One Foot?

This young vet was very helpful to me. As we talked he revealed that he had heard a similar idea from a horse chiropractor who regularly came to his school to lecture every year. The horse chiropractor believed that the spine held many secrets to horse lameness. Now, thanks to this gentleman's encouragement, the drive built up inside to pursue the theory to its conclusion. I realized that there were other people who cared as much as I did.

This young man actually wanted to specialize in lamenesses of the horse! And he wanted me to publish any information that I could on the subject. Today you are reading about my discovery and five years of research.

Pursuing The Wild Theory

Sore muscles can wreak havoc in the process of properly diagnosing the cause of a horse's lameness. Use of the plastic shoes for the sole

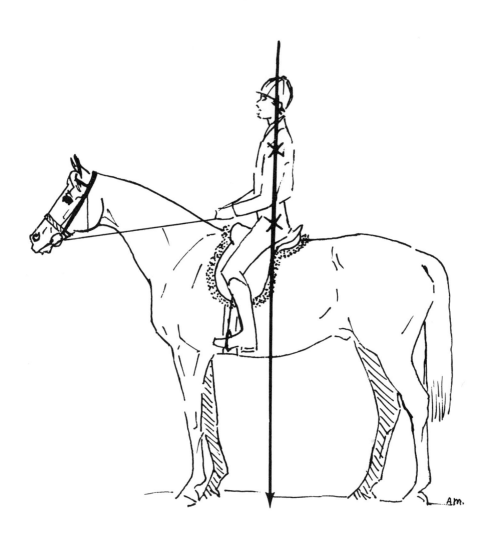

purpose of absorbing shock had no effect on the shoulder problem. The shoeing demonstrated that the horse's leg length or height, whichever way you want to look at it, has a definite effect on how a horse may get hurt while jumping. Also, a tight or sore muscle can be freed through shoeing. Psychologically, it was important to remember that one should not stop trying whatever method a farrier may try just because of criticism.

Leg Length Effect

A beautiful thing about trying new methods is that one learns from every experiment. No one ever knows the water is wet without jumping into it!

Dear Mr. Gonzales,

       The Wilton Pony Club would like to thank you for devoting your time for us. Our members are very interested and learned a great deal. We are working together to correct our ponies' problems. It is people like you who give up time, who make Pony Club a success. Thank you again.

       Sincerely,
       Marianne Frederick
       Secretary of Wilton Pony Club

Chapter 13

Ringbone
And
Spavin

Miss Clooney's Story

"It's my fault, I abused her!"

One of the most difficult parts of being a horseshoer is working with someone who has been abusing a horse. At best, one has to wonder what it is in people's minds that turns them into glory seekers—without any regard for an animal's well being. Psychology, at least as I learned

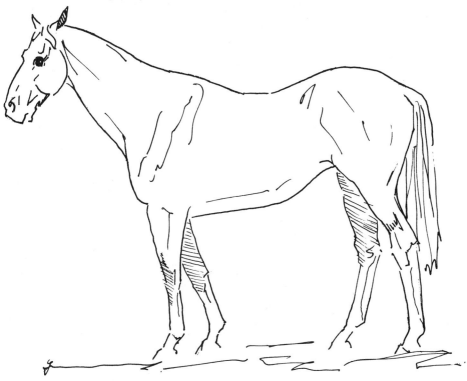

A Driving Ego

it in my first year of college, claims that ego can interfere with a person's reasoning. In many cases the ego establishes goals and is the driving force behind a person's ambitions. The process drives out all rational reasoning. I have seen enough examples of this kind to be comfortable with this explanation.

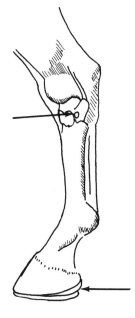

One day, I received a phone call from Mike. At first, there was nothing earthshaking, but what he was to ask me would send the hair on my neck straight up. "I have a 23-year-old mare, named Miss Clooney. Yes, she was named after the actress." Obviously he had been asked this question before and knew that I was going to ask the question. This told me that either this guy has ESP or a total lack of tolerance and patience. It didn't take long to learn which.

He continued, "It is all my fault. I abused her early on, in her prime. She can hardly get around now, but I heard that you can help her." Hearing this, the first thing that came to my mind was anger. It would have been easy to say, "Well, mister, if you were so dumb in not taking care of the horse, then you don't deserve to have

"It's All My Fault."

a horse." Then I caught myself and realized that I was not thinking about the horse's problem.

I pursued the questioning very diplomatically. What exactly is her problem? At this point, I sensed a change in his mood from defense to guilt. Keeping quiet, I still thought, "And I hope you can't sleep at night, too."

Miss Clooney had ringbone on both front

feet and a spavin on the right hind. Evidently, at this point, the medication was not having much effect on her. The owner wondered if there was anything that I could do to make her more comfortable.

People Control Horses

Situations like this tear at the horseshoer's heart. Why should I help an abuser clear his conscience? Still, making horses healthier and more comfortable is the farrier's purpose in life. The horse had been punished enough. I would help because the horse needed me.

People control horses, but only as keepers. When we work, test, or explore possibilities without logically considering the consequences, we can destroy another creature. The concern is awareness. Without it, horses will always be abused.

We made an appointment for Wednesday, at 3:30. I held a gut feeling there was going to be a pathetic sight when I made the appointment. This case was going to be hard for me, and I would have to put my true feelings behind me. As I drove to the appointment, I began thinking of ways to handle this situation. First I had to decide what I wanted to accomplish.

A Devil And An Angel

I felt like I was in a movie. Remember how a person would reason with himself—little image figures of the person as a devil and an angel sitting on opposite shoulders. I could refuse to have anything to do with Mike. That was the devil's side of it. Then the angel took its turn. If

Guilt: A Trap

you turn your back on the horse then you will be just as guilty.

No. I wouldn't be trapped by some imaginary do gooder. I did not put the animal in this situation.

One little figure promised guilt for not trying to help the horse. "If you find out after she gets put to sleep that you could have helped, then you will never hear the end of it from me. I won't let you rest."

"Don't listen."

"Remember your goal."

"Enough said. Back to reality," I told myself. As I arrived I saw a sad sight. If my resentment broke through, Mike would tell me to leave. There was no need for worry. My anger quickly turned into a desire to help Miss Clooney.

Stiff And In Pain

The mare was severely underweight. She walked very stiffly and showed signs of constant pain. It was going to be difficult to find something useful to do. Mike was embarrassed about the mare's condition. This was particularly evident from his chain smoking of cigarettes. As I got up to the horse, I couldn't avoid noticing the interest that was shown by the other boarders at this stable. The mixed human emotions of disgust and hope hung like clouds.

The mare was a grand lady. Her eyes

revealed her heart. She still had a lot of pride and she showed her spunk by squealing at a horse tied right next to her. "God love her," I thought to myself. Now it was time for me to put my emotions away and start thinking like a horseshoer. There had to be some solution. Clearly, whatever I did would be no cure. She was too far beyond that. The best that could still be done was to find some way to bring her relief from pain.

Positive Pain Elimination

At this point, I had seen how the work I was doing had some positive effect on eliminating pain. I had reached the conclusion that, if pain is present, then there must be a pressure point that is keeping the area always irritated. This pressure point was preventing the problem from healing fully.

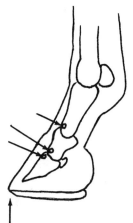

As I examined the mare, I found her stiff in the joint on all four legs. The ringbone on the front legs showed both high and low ringbone on the x-rays, according to Mike. I asked him to walk her on the lead line so I could get some idea how she moved. Then I noticed that the mare had the most severe problems with the right hind. The spavin was quite large. I asked Mike if the spavin came first or the ringbone. He indicated the ringbone.

Ringbone And Spavin Both

I then asked what type of work the mare had been doing. There was no way of guessing by this point. Mike stated she had been a rope horse, a calf roping as well as a team roping horse. That meant the mare would have to slide

Result Of Concussion

stop after the calf was caught at the end of the rope. This irritated the hocks, producing a spavin. When being used as a team horse, the mare would always have to turn with the steer. In many cases the rider would be riding out of the saddle, putting all his weight on the front end, producing added concussion.

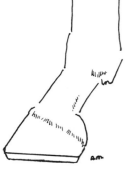

What did added concussion cause? Ringbone. It all started to make sense to me now.

Mike revealed to me that he had started calf roping first. Then, when he found that he could no longer do it, he turned to team roping. This mare had a heart of gold and she had started to go off when she was 13, but was able to give him four more years of pleasure before he could no longer ride her.

Can anyone doubt it is cruel to let a horse suffer this long? Even so, being human, I could see the sentiments that were projected here. Perhaps we all have felt that way about some animal in our lives.

Leather Pad Buffer

The best place to start was to find something to help the front legs cope with the shock of the hard ground. At the time, I had some very good, thick leather pads that would work as a buffer from concussion at the shoe. A rolled toe shoe was appropriate for both front feet. This was satisfactory. Now it was time to decide what to do about the hind.

While checking the mare's hind end for

equal balance of the hip muscles, I found that the right hind was shorter than the left. Up to this point, I had come to the conclusion that the movement of the shorter hind leg was generally abrupt. This would cause more concussion of the leg, especially since the shorter leg does not travel under the body as far as the longer leg. Because the joints of her hind legs were so stiff, it was very difficult for her to hold the leg up high when a handler lifted it. There had to be a way to make her comfortable without forcing too much pressure in the wrong areas. This required a considerable amount of time to think through, providing relief while taking into consideration the short leg.

Abrupt Leg Movement

It was possible that elevating her slightly in back, at the heels, would relieve some pressure in the hock and fetlock area. Then I could build up the right hind as well, to see if it would also help. In this case, it would be worth trying since she had already suffering from a lot of pain. I told Mike that I wanted to monitor the mare myself and that I would be down after work every day on my own just to satisfy my curiosity. It became an obsession.

Satisfying My Obsession

Each horseshoer, in the course of his work, runs across a horse which touches him very deeply. In this instance, there was also a matter of principle to prove. As the mare was taken away from me, I knew that she was heading back to a very lonely pasture, 200 acres to be precise. Her weight loss was related to her inability to roam the hills as well as she once could.

Satisfaction In Mike's Face

There was an air of satisfaction in Mike's face. It was not there because of the job I had done. Instead, he was satisfied because of what he did. He attempted to give her another chance through my work. This was the payback so to speak. I was glad that he felt that way but it still didn't quench my personal desire to help this mare. I could even detect a sigh of relief from the mare as she walked away from me.

For a moment I was convinced. "I did it, she's O.K." Then my cautious nature kicked in. It was far better to wait and see. I arrived the next day, asking directions to the mare's pasture. Mike had told me on the day before that he only came down to see the horse every other day. So I knew I would not run into him. The pasture was beautiful, full of trees and lush grass, but it was also a lonely place. I went through the gate and started to climb a hill. There was a thicket of trees where I thought she might be. She was right there. As I approached her, she seemed to be puzzled. It was as if she wanted to ask "What are you doing here?" I assured her that I had no intentions of catching her to ride. I just wanted to see how she was doing. I wasn't certain that she would believe me, so, just in case, I brought along some apples and a carrot as a persuasion. She took the bait.

Apple And Carrot Persuasion

She seemed to be a lot better in spirit, although I wasn't really certain. So I led her out

160

of the thicket. The next thing I knew, she trotted beside me. She was feeling much better. To my amazement, the next few times that I visited her she continually improved in spirit. You know that was worth seeing.

The Angel Was Right

There never was anything that I could do for the calcium deposits. Yet it was clear that the pain was lessening. The next few shoeings showed signs of loosening in the stiffness in her joints. Miss Clooney lived for another two years. She was even able to take Mike on small walking trail rides. She died of old age in pasture after a very wet winter. I felt good, knowing that she died with the least amount of pain in her legs that I could provide. The angel was right.

The age of a horse has no bearing on what horseshoers can do for a horse. People can be abusive to their horses and not really know it. Similarly the type of work can have a direct bearing on what lameness a horse will have.

Spavin was the real start of Miss Clooney's problem. In order to protect her hind end, the weight was transferred forward onto the front legs. Therefore the ringbone was actually a result of the spavin. When lameness shows up in front, nine times out of ten it is a result of a hind end compensation.

Great Falls Pony Club

Dear Tony,
    Just a small note to say how much
everyone from Great Falls Pony Club
enjoyed your lecture at the recent National
United States Pony Club Annual Meeting
in Philadelphia.
    It was interesting, informative and
very well presented. Thanks for taking
time off to go to the meeting. Everyone
benefited from you professional expertise!
    Sound feet and sound health to you
as always.

               Sincerely,
               Sue W. Elliott
               District Commissioner

Chapter 14

Moses' Story

"Let's balance one and leave
the other one alone."

The Start Of A Theory

Most customers fail to credit my brother with a clever mind, but he certainly has one. Moses and I started on this theory together. I studied a little harder and followed the implications a lot farther than Moses did, but we discovered the idea together and it was Moses' idea to call the philosophy and shoeing technique, Proper Balance Movement (P.B.M).

Both Moses and I knew that the work we had done with lame horses was phenomenal. But we were also concerned about the sound horse. What could P.B.M. teach about a young horse? What would happen if we could take a young horse and balance it before its training.?

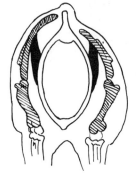

Moses and I discovered that when we balanced lame horses, their attitudes also changed. We had seen horses, when relieved from pain and the constant fear of pain, totally change their personalities. Horses became more docile, more willing to work. In many ways they showed their gratitude for their relief.

An Untrained Horse

A worthwhile chance to see how P.B.M. would work on an untrained horse finally presented itself. Moses and my sister Margaret had bought two young geldings from a breeder on the big island. Both colts were sired by the same stallion and essentially had the same conformation.

Moses did the usual ground breaking of the colts, until they got used to the weight of the saddle on their backs. Then they underwent the bitting process, which involves leaving the bit in the colt's mouth. This allows colts to get used to having it in their mouths without throwing their heads or playing with the bits. Bitting is a very satisfactory way to get a head start on the training process.

Bitting

Neither horse had shoes. We decided to leave them that way for a few weeks to see how they progressed in the training. One colt was a chestnut and the other was a bay. Both colts possessed good personalities. Both colts had similar builds. Each was uneven in the front legs, and higher in the right shoulder. Both colts had been put out to pasture all this time, eating only grass and no grain, so weight was held to a minimum. The colts actually had more muscle tone and firmer bodies as a result of living on the mountainside.

We found that the natural climbing up and down the sides of mountains gave our horses much more natural balance. They had to get used to standing in all kinds of positions to eat grass. Hilly pasture also helps prevent a horse from being built downhill. The animal has to lift its front end up in order to go uphill. Therefore, the withers will be allowed to stretch upward. This stretches the muscles in between the shoulder blade and the chest cavity to the maximum.

Mountains For Balance

As Moses trained the colts, I watched him work them every day to observe the progress that they were making. Both colts were level headed at first, but the chestnut started to lose his good nature.

Off To A Fighting Start

The attitude change was noticeable after two weeks of being ridden. He started to fight everything Moses was trying to do. By this time I had figured out what was happening, but I wanted to make sure we gave the colt the full opportunity to develop his bad temper before we did anything.

Three Days Of Rest

I checked his feet to see if there was any bruising. Then I checked the colt's back to see if he was sore anywhere. No sign of any problems there. Finally, in order to give the chestnut a chance to regain his temper before I balanced him, I asked Moses to let him rest for three days. Admittedly, this set his training off schedule, but it was important to remove all possibile causes for this colt's attitude change. In addition, he had started falling down to the right periodically.

There were times up to this point when both Moses and I thought that this colt was just hardheaded, and that he was actually throwing himself down to the right as a protest. But we were proved wrong. When he went down, Moses would sit as the colt lay on the ground and think about what the horse had done.

Falling Down, Falling Down

There was reason to suspect that this wasn't a temper tantrum. The colt would never fight Moses while lying on the ground on his side. It was as if he were relieved not to have

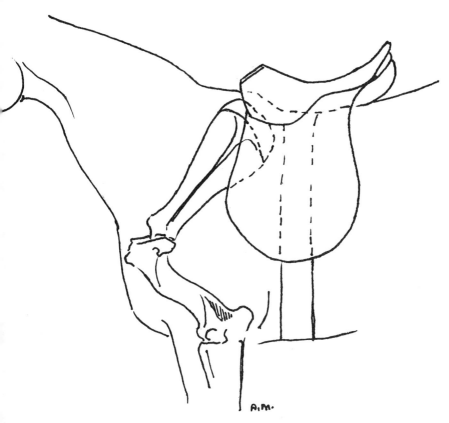

someone on his back. Meanwhile the bay colt
was progressing at a steady rate. His development was nothing to burn up the world, but on
the other hand there was adequate progress.
After two weeks the bay was now neck reining **Adequate**
with some efficiency, he would stop on his hind **Progress**
end rather than his front, and his trot and canter
were satisfactory. This progress was far better
than the chestnut colt's.

One could sense the insecurity in the

167

A Reevaluation

chestnut's turns and stops. He would bounce the rider up when he stopped. After three days of rest, Moses and I reevaluated the chestnut colt. There was no change. In fact, he fell again. Moses was becoming frustrated. I convinced him that it was my turn to take over the training. First, I examined the saddle, and found that it was sitting down on the right shoulder blade. This would explain why he fell when Moses directed him to turn to the right. Moses placed more weight in his right stirrup, thereby pushing harder on the right shoulder. The saddle was pinching the shoulder blade so hard, it caused enough pain to make the animal collapse.

First, The Saddle

Removing the saddle I started to press on the shoulder blade where the colt appeared to be tender. I received the response I was expecting. The colt threw back his ears and tried to get away from me. He was definitely sore. The most logical starting place appeared to be the colt's front end. If more balancing was needed, we could work on the hind end. Just the same I wanted to take care of one end at a time.

I raised the chestnut colt's left front leg one half of an inch. This brought his shoulders to where they were reasonably level. I also placed another saddle pad on his back in order to take up more of the concussion of the rider.

Now the true test remained.

These two colts were to be rope horses. Good rope horses have to be able to turn without

168

falling down. Actually, the chestnut colt would be suitable for a right handed roper, because this roper always turns a steer off to the left. He would also be satisfactory as a calf horse, provided that the calf always ran straight. The only thing that the right handed roper couldn't do with the colt would be to lean out of the saddle to the right. His weight on the right shoulder would make the colt fall. For a left hander, this colt would be a disaster. The left handed roper always turns off to the right.

A Satisfactory Calf Horse, Sometimes

Now after shoeing and repadding under the saddle, we put the chestnut colt back into a slow training program. I decided that I wanted the colt to be lunged on the lead line first before placing anyone on his back. We would try him at a canter both ways, then back down to a walk, then trot. This allows whatever tight muscles the horse has to stretch, then to extend to maximum length, then contract down to a walk. By this time the stride will have increased, because of the loose muscles.

Americans have a tendency to bring their horses out of the stall, saddle them up, and start them off walking. Then the rider trots the animal to exhaustion, canters a little, and puts the animal back in its stall. By this point, the horse has just relaxed and stretched all his muscles, and then he is returned to his stall.

Moses and I had a nice, small arena where we trained the colts. However, rather than let them become bored, we would take them on

Improving On Turns

trailrides up and down hills. After the first workout, we noticed a difference. The colt seemed to have more confidence. Also he started improving on his turns to the right. There had been no sign of the chestnut colt attempting to fall down.

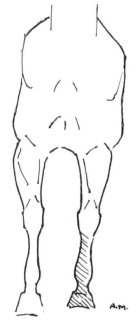

Obviously there had not been enough testing to reach a confident conclusion, so we decided to stick to the program of progressive training. This started with half hour workouts, leading up to one hour of intensive riding in two weeks. As the weeks progressed, new ideas on training and muscle development progress began to occur to me. I came up with the idea that these colts should learn to step over poles on the ground. This would allow the leg muscles to stretch forward. As the leg muscles stretch and develop, the stride increases.

I would have the colts walk between two poles lying on the ground. Then we would turn them sharply either way, forcing the horse not only to pick the leg up faster but also to stretch his chest muscles from side to side. As the chest muscles develop, they provide a more confident motion, so the colt begins to negotiate his turns fluidly.

Stepping Over Poles

Later we took some trees that had blown down and placed them across a stretch of trail. This made the horses pick their legs up as an exercise. I had all these exercises performed at a walk. The walk is a committed motion which demands that the horse pick up his leg and stretch it, up and forward, which produces the

170

maximum effect. There is convincing evidence that without the momentum of the trot and canter, the horse develops much more quickly. Anyone who lifted weights, either for power or body building, will testify that the maximum effect comes with slow and methodical exercise. What we were doing here with these two colts was actually going to answer some very important questions that I had been curious about for years. Only by testing my theory with two quite similar young horses, could I get a satisfactory and worthwhile answer.

Slow, Methodical Exercise

Why does a horse sometimes have a hard time taking one lead? This resistance seems to be a frequent problem with many horses. Why does a horse cut in one direction, but resists and becomes stiff when turned the other way? Why do young horses sometimes respond well in the beginning stages of their training and then become idiots? Why do horses stumble? Why do horses seem to have their rear ends fall out from under them? Most importantly, why do horses go lame in one foot first, and then, eventually, in the other? This is the mystery of one legged lameness.

The chestnut colt quickly stopped fighting Moses. This showed me that, psychologically, the balance shoeing had an effect on the colt. He excelled in his training exercises, showing security in his motion. This security demonstrated that the colt's fear of falling was now gone. He could execute his turns both ways fluently. As far as his leads were concerned, there was no

The Psychological Effect

171

longer a bad side. He was able to change leads in mid air. The chestnut actually caught up with the bay colt's training in two weeks. Perhaps the most remarkable part of this success was his speed in learning.

A Fast Learner

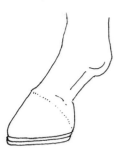

In fact, he learned so fast that after a month had gone by, we evaluated both colts and decided to balance the bay colt. Up to this point, the bay had done well but we wanted to see if he could catch up to the chestnut now. When we balanced him, he caught up.

Moses and I had stumbled into a new enhancement of training techniques. Both colts became good rope horses. After wearing the lifts for three shoeings, we shod them normally. We never had to balance them again. By the way, the bay had to be lifted in the left front one quarter of an inch, later reduced to one eighth of an inch.

When a horse needs to be balanced for movement, the shoeing technique is just temporary. Only when the animal is lame will one sometimes need to keep a lift on the animal. Even this lift is usually at a reduced height. When I speak of a lift, I mean a pad between the shoes and the hoof. In this case I used a rim pad.

Training Enhancement

In training these colts, Moses said that he did not have to use as much repetition as he was accustomed to. I now knew that balancing is an important part of a young horse's training. Balancing includes analyzing the horse's saddle, rider, and shoeing. We have to be aware of the effect any change or addition will have on young horses. Additionally, we must learn to read the signs that the horses are showing us. This will save us from frustration and from possible lameness in the future. Riding and training are definite factors in understanding the causes of, and solutions to, lameness.

The Saddle, The Rider, The Shoe

Dear Tony,

    I'm the person who brought the dressage horse to your clinic in St. Louis. I just wanted to again tell you how much I enjoyed receiving this new knowledge. You're right, I could really relate to this because all of the matters you touched upon are very pointedly related to dressage.

    I have always said there are no "bad" horses and they only act that way because they hurt (unless their training or treatment has been brutal, etc.) I haven't found a person in the world to agree with me yet but your clinic certainly confirmed that for me.

    I thought I knew my horse's body as well as anyone could and really feel stupid not even knowing one shoulder is bigger than the other and one more forward, etc.

    I am so thankful my shoer is interested in your methods.

                      Sincerely,
                      Nancy Kutta

Chapter 15

Fancy's Story

"My pony has a splint that is always hot after I jump her!"

A Hot Splint On The Left

I received a call from a frustrated mother. Several treatments had been used to heal a splint on the left leg of her daughter's pony. They had tried everything from blisters to shoeing. There was no improvement. In fact, it was getting bigger.

It was hard to understand what she wanted me to do when everything had already been tried. Then she said something that really grabbed my curiosity. Apparently, whenever they jumped the pony, when the pony was brought back to the barn the splint would be hot. Now I had a few questions to ask.

Could the problem be related to the horse's body heat? No, because the splint stayed hot long after the pony's body cooled. Was the ground too hard? No, the ring was kept disked. Had hoof pads been used as cushions? Yes, but they didn't make any difference. Then she hit me with a bombshell. "My vet had asked me to call you, to see if you could shed some light on what is happening. He has heard of your work and wants your opinion."

On The Spot

I was flattered, but it was clear this pair was also putting me on the spot. They needed help and I could not refuse. Besides, this was a situation that I had not encountered before. This really looked like a challenge. In fact, even if I couldn't find all the answers right away, this could be a real education.

By this time I had established my approach

to each new case. Start by watching the rider on the horse. Then look at the horse's conformation. Finally, choose the most efficient way to balance the horse by shoeing. This was working from the top down instead of from the bottom up.

From The Top Down

I watched the little girl ride her horse in a big stable where there was plenty of activity. Somehow, it still seemed as if this new case of mine was the center of all attention. I guess it is hard for people to accept that a horseshoer can understand a lot about the horse and rider.

Watching this lovely grey pony named Fancy, and her proud owner Tara, I could see that they were well suited to meet each other's needs. A worried look came over the young owner's face when I asked to see the pony jump a few fences. I needed to know how the pony approached the fences before I could determine if the rider was contributing to the problem.

When I entered the ring, Tara was walking the pony. As the pony walked down the rail away from me, I noticed that Tara was leaning toward the right. It looked as if she were struggling to stay upright in the saddle. Also, Tara would drop her left shoulder down to the left, cocking her head to the left as well. Then when the pony began to trot, the falling to the right became worse.

The Rider's Contribution

Tara's mother had mentioned her concern about her daughter's riding posture. She

177

commented that her child had a problem sitting straight in the saddle. She was apparently convinced that Tara was responsible for her own crookedness.

A Switched Lead

A.m.

Pinching Saddle

When Fancy began to approach the jump, she started off on the right lead. Then, as she got ready to take off, she lifted off. But she switched to the left lead when she landed. This was unusual. The pony also threw the left leg out farther than normal to the left. When I had seen enough, we returned to the barn. As the child rode to the barn, I was walking behind, talking with her mother.

I pointed out to the mother that Tara was leaning to the right. Then I pointed out to her how much lower the right shoulder was, in relation to the left stirrup. This surprised her. At that point, I showed them how to check the saddle, to see if it was sitting on a shoulder blade. If it were, it could interfere with the horse's normal movement. This can be checked by putting a hand underneath the saddle and saddle padding in front of the saddle. I started with the right front. Here, I could slide my hand in and out very easily. Then I checked the left side. I couldn't even get my hand under the pad. Obviously, the saddle was pinching the pony's left shoulder blade.

When I showed this procedure to my two clients, they were astounded. No one had pointed this out before. After taking the saddle off the pony, I showed them how the conformation of

the pony was the major contributing factor to
Tara's inability to hold her balance.

Now the first procedure in reading a horse
is to stand behind the hindquarters and assess
the shape of the withers and shoulders. In this
case, the pony's left shoulder was overdeveloped. The right shoulder blade was much lower
than the left. The left shoulder blade appeared
to be what I call a roll over shoulder. This means
that if one measured the distance from the
shoulder blade to the top of the withers on each
side, one side would be closer to the withers than
the other. Also, the angle of the withers would
be tilted toward the lower side. In this case, the
withers sloped toward the right shoulder blade.

In assessing the hind end, I discovered
that the right hind leg was longer than the left
hind leg. This can be determined by the shape of
the muscles and also by feeling the top of the hip
horns—where the spine goes through.

The next step is to look at the pony from
the side. In this instance, the pony's hind end
was slightly higher than the front. So, in analyzing the pony's conformation, there were three
long legs and one short leg. The right hind was
the longest leg, with the left front second longest.

After this, it is necessary to analyze what
the motion was all about. The height of the
pony's legs caused a diagonal leg problem. So the
movement of the legs would be as follows. Starting with the longest leg, the right hind leg was

Diagonal Movement

stepping in under the pony's body. Remember, in order to drop the hip to become level, by the nature of this motion the pony would push the right cheek of Tara's buttocks up and forward. This movement, in turn, would send Tara's weight diagonally forward onto the pony's left shoulder. The weight would be transferred from the right cheek of her buttocks onto her left knee. The left knee would jam forward into the left shoulder.

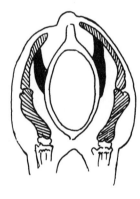

Since the left shoulder was higher, the pony's leg motion would swing to the outside, producing a shorter stride due to the interference of the saddle. This movement would then shift Tara's position, by forward momentum, onto the right shoulder. As the right shoulder had to extend farther forward in order to maintain balance, Tara's weight would then shift to the ball of her right foot, pushing the right foot forward and causing her to fall over to the right. This tendency to fall to the right was increased by the shoulder being lower and the lack of muscle support for the saddle. Tara's reaction to losing her balance would now be to push herself back to the left. This time, the weight would be

A Backward Thrust

sent to the left cheek of her buttocks, forcing the pony's right hind leg to shorten its movement to support the rider's weight. Otherwise, Tara would fall off the horse toward the right rear.

This sounds like quite a lot of motion and weight shifting, but actually I have just described what happened to Fancy and Tara when all four legs moved forward only one step. How did all of this shifting affect the pony's splint problem?

Pain Reduction

The pony was getting hit in the shoulder by the forward momentum of the rider, launched by the right hind leg. To help reduce her pain, Fancy would throw her left front leg to the outside of her body. Throwing the leg to the outside did reduce the pressure on the shoulder from the rider's weight, but it caused the stride to shorten as well. This shortened stride also thrust the rider onto the right shoulder. When this happened, the left front leg's push actually came from the inside of the leg, thus putting constant pressure on the irritated inner splint. This was why the splint bone was hot after every jumping session.

Frustration

When all this was explained to Tara and her mother, Tara said that she had known her saddle posture was not her fault. However, her instructor spent most of the time during her lessons screaming at her to sit up in the saddle. It had reached the point where Tara was beginning to get frustrated with riding and losing her hope of ever becoming a good rider.

Now for the next question. How should one shoe a horse for this problem?

I had determined that the horse's problem leg was the right hind, but the left front leg had the problem of the splint. The right hind leg was doing what I call weight transferral onto the left front. This weight transferral is the result of

Compression Strains

an underlying problem, which in this case was a sore stifle in the right hind leg. The left front leg was breaking down because of its inability to handle the compression strains, with the rider's weight adding to this problem.

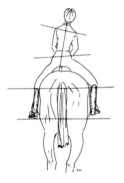

The first step in a case like this is to assess how much difference there is in the length of the legs. I put my hand on the withers with all four fingers flat on top. Then I take my thumb and feel for the top of the shoulder blade. After I find it, I take the little finger of my hand and probe the other side for the top of the shoulder blade on that side. This gives me some idea of how far I need to go. Then I place pads under the hoof in order to see how far I am off. If the horse has shoes on, I take the shoe off the longer leg. If it is still too high at the shoulders, then I cut the foot. This gives a good idea of what one is dealing with in terms of how much to build up.

Never The First Time

It is important to remember that one never balances a horse evenly the first time. Muscles need to relax and stretch without being forced. Never radically balance a horse that is not lame, especially if one is not experienced at balancing. A sound horse should not be raised more than one quarter inch. A lame horse can be raised as much as two inches. Always use pads or rim pads to raise the leg. Always use flat pads. Flat pads will not throw the positions of the joint out of balance. The pads will give the leg more cushion to add to the capacity of the muscle to absorb concussion.

This method of shoeing is a constant learning process. It took me one year to discover the theory, five years to perfect prevention awareness, and it will take me a lifetime to find answers to all the questions and situations I find. The information in this book is only part of the picture. Anyone who reads this book and believes he is an expert is a fool. This book is only part of the teaching. New exceptions to the exceptions will confuse one all the time. That's why it is necessary to understand the whole picture. One example appears in the next chapter.

A Constant Learning Process

Now in shoeing Fancy, I estimated that the pony was three quarters of an inch off on the right front leg. Then I estimated that the left hind was off one quarter of an inch. I raised the right front one half inch. This was done by using two quarter inch thick leather pads. I made the surface side full and the inner pad a rim, and packed the foot with silicone. I raised the left hind leg with a plastic rim pad that was an eighth of an inch thick. Then I applied a rolled toe shoe on both hind feet to ease breakover.

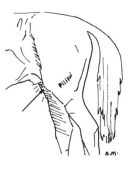

Tara's mother was told to place more padding under the saddle, especially over the withers. The two were told to canter the pony for five minutes, turning in each direction before any workouts, in order to loosen up muscles.

The Whole Picture

I heard objections to putting pads on one side, because the owners felt that the weight might interfere with the horse's movement, or throw the horse off balance. These objections

Redirecting The Stress

were easily answered by pointing out the standard treatment for a horse with an abcess in the sole or frog of one foot. Most veterinarians prescribe putting on one pad to allow the foot to heal, but very rarely will they prescribe pads for both front feet because of concerns about weight or balance. Afterwards, most horses go off, becoming sound without experiencing movement problems because of only having one pad on one foot. This normally ends any argument.

Padding, when used to properly balance leg length, will act as height for the leg and length for the stride. In many cases where minimal pain is evident, the shoeing will be temporary. The lift can be taken off once the muscles of the leg develop sufficiently to sustain the needed height of the leg, redirecting the stress in the affected area. When carefully monitored, the problem usually won't come back.

Awareness is the key to success. If the horseowner does not understand what he should do to help the healing process, don't expect a miracle. Also, don't be quick to blame the shoeing method if you do not know the whole picture. Horseshoeing and riding take a lifetime to learn. No one can ever know it all.

The Key To Success

A final thought on Fancy's problem. The splint would not have been as bad if Tara had not had a shorter right leg also. Think about it. With padding, the splint actually reduced in size. Soon it was hardly noticable. The owners were able to compete heavily and also fox hunt with the pony, with no sign of a recurring problem. Eventually I lost track of Fancy, when the owners sold her for big money.

No Recurring Problem

Center of gravity

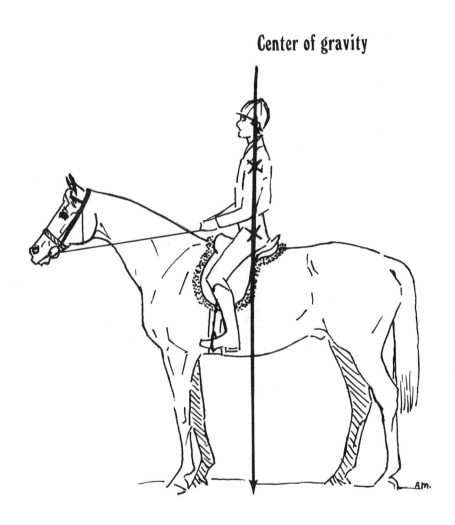

Mr. Gonzales,

My blacksmith was at your lecture this spring and he came back so excited about your PBM that he left reprints of the article that appeared in the *Farrier's Journal*.

I have a thoroughbred lay-up farm and you can bet your boots I have every kind of hoof problem and lameness problem imaginable. My blacksmith (Don Tritz) and I have worked together on each and every horse and have seen fantastic results which are only destroyed when the horses return to the truck. WHACK! off come the heels and out go the toes—whether they need it or not. We have looked at all of the horses here and have analyzed them according to your ideas. If only we had the time to do right by the horse.

Thank you for passing on your ideas.

Sincerely,
Linda F. Beyer

Chapter 16

Marsha's Story

**"She twists over her jumps and bucks
when she gets to the other side."**

As my motion and rider analysis theories took shape and began to gain acceptance, life turned exciting. Referrals became more interesting. One special call came from a riding instructor. Marsha was a respected expert at training jumpers and she needed help with a mare.

I gladly accepted the challenge, especially

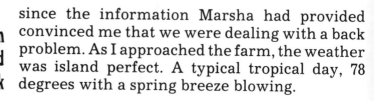
An Old Milk Container

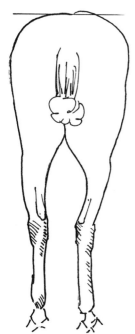

Difficult To Work With

since the information Marsha had provided convinced me that we were dealing with a back problem. As I approached the farm, the weather was island perfect. A typical tropical day, 78 degrees with a spring breeze blowing.

Marsha greeted me and led me to the mare's stall. She was a big thoroughbred mare, about 16 hands high. For Hawaii, this was a tall horse. As Marsha brought the mare out of the stall, I looked for something to stand on, to get a good view of the shoulders and withers from over the hind end and found an old milk container.

While she stood the mare up, Martha started to tell me some of the horse's history. The mare was nine years old, and she had been jumping for five years. Most of the mare's experience was at the three foot level. Marsha now wanted the mare to jump three feet nine inches and higher. The mare had been performing well for the first six months, winning her competitions. However, lately, she had become difficult to work with. The mare started to resist her rider's leaning, to change her lead and buck on the other side of the fence.

This horse had a similar build to Fancy, the pony I described in an earlier chapter. The left shoulder was more developed, and the right shoulder sat lower. The right hind leg was longer and the left hind leg lower. The side view revealed that the hind end was slightly higher, about the same conformation that the pony had.

However, the mare differed in one symptom. She had no splint problem. There was a lump on the left side of the back. It felt as if a vertebra could be rising.

A Lump On The Back

Marsha saddled the mare, to allow an assessment of the saddle position. As in Fancy's case, the saddle rested in the left shoulder area. I could not get my hand under the saddle from the left side, but over the right shoulder area I could reach in. From a rear view, the riderless saddle was leaning over to the right shoulder. The seat of the saddle shifted so it was sitting more on the right side of the back.

Marsha mounted the mare's back and adjusted the saddle by shifting her weight toward the left. Significantly Marsha was not aware that she shifted her weight to the ball of her right foot automatically when mounting the horse. Her next reaction was to shove the weight back onto the left cheek bone of her buttocks. This shift of weight was causing the saddle to rub the bump of the back, causing the mare always to move about whenever Marsha would mount her. This was another complaint that concerned Marsha.

What happened to this horse when she and her rider jumped over a fence? I watched the horse move on the flat. Her best direction was to the left. Why should this be? To the right, the mare's head would pull forward and her ears would go back. Then she would ring her tail after she came out of her corners. Why?

Go Left

189

Switching, Twisting, Bucking

As the mare approached a jump, her ears would go forward, but as soon as she got into the jump, her ears would go back, and she would switch her leads from right to the left. Then she would land on her left lead, twisting her back in mid air. This way, she tried to push her rear end to the right, then buck, after landing with all four feet on the ground. Marsha was baffled about what she could do. The horse no longer responded to a beating. Also, the mare got worse when Marsha did try to correct the behavior. Practice sessions had reached the point where the mare was beginning to refuse sometimes, usually after a few times around a course.

Marsha knew the mare was in pain, but there were no outward signs that anyone could identify. As we returned to the barn, I suggested to Marsha that the root of the problem appeared clear to me. When we reached the barn, Marsha placed her hand under the back of the saddle to feel where the bump was, in relation to the saddle. I walked the mare away from her so that she could watch how, when the mare walked, the saddle shifted from side to side. Most importantly, she could see the saddle slipping more to the right, stopping about where the bump rose on the back.

Riding Position

Following the demonstration, I explained her riding position to Marsha. She agreed that she had found herself dropping her left shoulder and forcing herself to stay upright in the saddle, trying to avoid falling to the right. Marsha had believed this problem was due to her short leg

190

being the right leg. I then presented to her the riding scenario with this mare.

As Marsha was going into her jumps, her riding position would fall on the right shoulder. Then as she sat up for departure, her weight would move toward the left rear. This placed her weight right on the area of the bump. The mare would change her lead in order to get the rider off her back, twisting to try to keep the rider moving towards the right. Then Marsha would react to this by sitting back to the left rear. This caused the mare to buck, in order to thrust the rider up off the bump. This was also the reason the mare's best side was the left. Marsha was able to stay up in the saddle, thrusting her weight back to the right rear, where there was no bump to cause pain. When she moved to the right, the saddle shifted and her weight would push back towards the left rear, putting pressure on the bump.

How should one shoe for this problem? In this case, I did not know how effective balance shoeing would be, because I had never before encountered a horse with this problem. Finding a method to correct the weight shifts and protect a popped vertebra really made me stop and think. The greatest problem was the bump.

Correct Weight Shifts

I reexamined the back carefully. The spine, along the left side of the back, seemed to protrude up toward the point of the bump. There also was a change, more like a curvature of the spine from that point on to the hip, where

Curvature Of The Spine

it seemed higher on the opposite side. Other horses I balanced probably had some curvature to their spines, but I couldn't see the curvature because of their build. On this mare, the curvature was obvious, so I took a chance.

The mare's right shoulder appeared to be lower than the left by at least three quarters of an inch. The left hind leg was off no more than a quarter of an inch. In this case, the mare had three nearly even long legs and one short leg. The judgment was a little tricky for me, because this horse was actually sound. The mare was showing some signs of motion lameness, so I proceeded to balance the legs. I put a half inch rim pad on her right front leg. Then I used a rim shoe in front, with a slight rolled toe. The reasoning behind this was to give the mare security with grabbing of the ground in front, while enabling her to break over with ease. She was given an eighth of an inch pad on the left hind leg. This was just a rim pad, with heeled shoes in back, and no rolled toe. When I finished, Marsha was astounded.

It's Gone!

What we both saw was unbelievable. The bump had disappeared. Marsha saddled the mare and took her back to the ring, to see if there was a change in how she moved or reacted to leads to the right, and to see if the bump would reappear. I checked the saddle to see if there was any pressure. When one more pad was added to the saddle, the left shoulder had room to move one's hand in and out. We took the mare to the ring, and the mare behaved just as she had earlier when Marsha tried to mount her. This was predictable, but what was to come was really unexpected.

No Switching, No Bucking

Marsha rode the mare around the ring at a canter first, then a walk. Finally she rode at a trot. The mare showed no sign of a drastic improvement, although there was some noticeable change in her movement. I asked Marsha to jump the mare over a few jumps. As Marsha came into the first fence, the mare gave the same approach. She switched her lead over the fence, but when she landed there wasn't much of a twist. The mare did not buck. Also, Marsha was not rotating her body from front to back. Then, when they both came to the next fence, the mare did not switch her lead and there was no buck. Marsha took her over three more jumps and the mare did not twist, change leads or buck. It was as if she had been cured.

Looking For Answers

Marsha went on to win many classes with this mare and the problem never came back. I learned a valuable lesson that day. Balance shoeing was even able to correct a problem in the horse's back. This case had caused me to search for more answers. Later I received confirmation from two very reliable equine researchers that horses have curvatures in their spines. This curvature has a substantial effect on the horse when it develops unevenly from side to side. Also, the shoeing technique allows the

193

**Curved
Spine
Pressure** muscles that are overstretched to relax, muscles that are underdeveloped to develop, and helps relieve the pressure of the curved spine, allowing it to realign.

Chapter 17

Philosophy

What is my philosophy of shoeing?

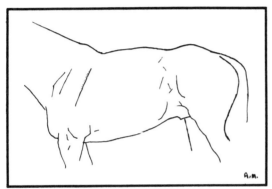

24. Roached Back

Shoeing can either be a help or a hindrance. Intelligent shoeing helps horses that need corrective shoeing. However, incomplete knowledge of corrective shoeing is dangerous in the hands of a person who doesn't really understand the proper use of every method and type of shoe. An inexperienced horseshoer attempting Proper Balance Movement techniques could cause irreversible damage in some cases. This makes continual education absolutely essential for horseowners and horseshoers.

More people need to question why things are done a certain way. They need to reach their own conclusions. Research in this country is limited in all fields of the horse world. Veterinary and riding training and most of all horseshoeing education is limited and occasionally incomplete. Everyone waits for someone else to make an improvement in teaching methods. This book is just a small step forward. We need to make a lot more progress.

Horseshoeing needs to incorporate knowledge from many fields, including anatomy of the whole horse, kinesiology (the study of motion), physics, orthopedics, the psychology of both horse and owner, practical therapy techniques, and business. Many horseshoers have already developed skill in these fields of study, even without knowing it. Today horseshoeing is a science. It is no longer a trade.

Mathematical Formulas

Farriers have mathematical formulas for making shoes. We use properties of physics in determining torque, compression, concussion, and force which come into play when a horse puts its foot on the ground. Similarly horseshoers use kinesiology when observing the motion of the leg moving through the air.

Orthopedic Principles

Orthopedic principles govern every application of pads to horses—whether for protection or to increase or decrease the hoof angle. Psychology is an important part of making a horse comfortable and handling the attitude changes of both horse and owner. Practical therapy techniques vary from the application of linament to the preservation of many horseowners' only source of mental escape from the pressure of the real world—the horse. Business is putting food on the table.

There is more to the farrier's job than just shoeing horses.

Here is an introduction to the basic principles underlying the science of horseshoeing.

Front lower leg lameness makes a good starting place. Occasionally a foot is cut too short. This is always accidental. There are several ways of desensitizing a foot. One can apply a hot shoe to burn the cut.

The method I prefer is to mix iodine crystals and turpentine. Put the iodine crystals on the sole and pour a capful of turpentine on the crystals. This will cause a chemical reaction that will cause the crystals to melt with an intense heat. When using this method, the hoof should be wrapped very tightly so none of the liquid spills down the hairline. The mixture will burn the hair severely and yield a noxious smoke that can cause nausea when inhaled. The procedure is dangerous for the horse and may scare him. Only experienced people should do this if it is at all necessary.

Experienced People Only

Mothballs are another effective treatment. Put mothballs on the hoof and apply a hot shoe to burn the mothballs. This forms a coating as well.

Sometimes it's better to use simple methods like applying formaldehyde, the chemical used to preserve animal experiments in school science classes. Pour some on the sole. Then at night use a pine tar pack, consisting of cotton and pine tar.

Quicking: Sensitive And Pressure

There are two types of quicking with an nail, sensitive quicking and pressure quicking. Sensitive quicking involves actually driving the nail into the sensitive laminae of the foot. One will generally get a reaction from the horse and blood oozing out from the top of the nail hole. In most cases pulling the nail and treating the hole with iodine and soaking will heal the problem. In contrast, pressure quicking is when a nail is driven close to the sensitive tissue but not into it. The irritation here comes when the hoof itself expands as the horse puts its foot on the ground. The nail will rub against the tissue. When this happens, all one must do is pull the nail and reset a new nail in a better position. It is easy to tell the difference between the two quicks, because the sensitive quick, if not caught, will yield heat and even swelling the next day. Also, the horse will become lame each day it is not attended to. On the other hand, I have had people call me five days later telling me that I quicked their horses— only for us to discover stone bruises.

Ringbone

Ringbone, according to tradition, gets its name from the presence of calcium around the short pastern and long pastern bones. The round shape caused it to be called a ring. In the cases I have seen, the calcium has usually been on the front of the bones. Ringbone normally points to a problem originating from concussion. Horses with ringbone often have straighter pasterns, which create more pressure in the center of the joints. Therefore, to improve the angle, I use a rolled toe shoe and then bevel the outer ground surface of the shore all the way around. This gives the animal the benefit of rotating its pastern whichever way makes the horse more comfortable. I also use rim pads to buffer the shock received from hitting the ground. In some cases I raise the heels as well.

Shoeing a horse with sidebone is virtually the same as shoeing for ringbone, except for beveling the outside ground surface of the shoe. This avoids creating any more pressure on the affected area when the horse has to make a turn. **Sidebone**

Navicular is one of the most severe problems. There may be two different problems with pressure that create navicular. One originates with pressure from the back angle of the foot. The other comes from the front angle of the foot. The navicular horse that responds to bar shoe and angle raises has the pastern joints set back from the coronet band. Therefore, if the angle is too far down, the pressure of the tendon creates irritation of the navicular bone. On the other hand, the horse that does not respond to bar shoes and angle raises has pastern joints that are more upright and short, and are set closer to the coronary band. Bar shoes and angle raises only increase the irritation. The pressure comes from the hoof wall pushing against the coffin short pastern joint. This pushes the navicular bone against the tendon. Rubbing of the navicular **Pressure-Created Navicular**

A Test For Navicular

bone against the tendon creates irritation to the navicular bone and to the coffin joint as well. To check whether the horse has this problem, place the thumb about one half inch above the coronary band, and push in. If soreness is present, the horse will pop his foot right up in the air as soon as he is touched. One word of warning, don't test for soreness while directly in front of the horse. You will be hit in the face or head by the horse's knee. Perform this test from the side. Also, make sure to not use a fingernail to test for this. All horses will react to a fingernail, whether they have navicular or not.

I will discuss founder in a later book.

Tendons And Ligaments

What is the best way to deal with bowed tendons, and suspensary, ligament problems? If these problems are caught in the beginning, with higher angle changes to relieve stress on the afflicted area, when healing occurs the angles can be decreased to a lower angle at a slow rate. Use of wedged pads and rolled toes can be effective. The rocker toe shoes on the front do not keep the foot on the ground for a long period of time. This reduces the pressure on the afflicted area.

The Hind End

Now turn to hind leg problems, stifle, hock (spavins), and pulled tendons. Stifle symptoms usually are the result of a movement problem. A horse can slip forward with each movement of the leg, causing a greater strain on the joint. The horse can also have the leg catch

200

behind itself. In order to help the joint, the pressure from leg motion must not be allowed to get to the point of strain. I usually raise the heels using heeled shoes, with the height depending on how bad the problem is. For severe problems I use wedge pads. Always keep rolled toe shoes on the hind end. Most horses that are prone to stifle problems have pointed hooves in the hind feet. So, along with the rolled toe shoes, try to round the hooves.

Hock problems are mostly spavins. Most spavined horses have low heels in the hind feet. **Spavins** Normally, they also have stiff hocks, with no flexion. The real cause of spavins is insufficient use of the hock joint and overuse of the fetlock joint. When the fetlock joint shuffles the leg forward, it prevents the hock joint from opening as much as it should. Here, it helps to raise the heels, as well as to use the rocker toe shoe. In these cases it is best only to use flat shoes and wedge pads.

Tendon problems in the hind end are usually a result of very sloping pasterns. This severe **A** angle creates a sickle-like hock stance and pushes **Severe** the cannon bone behind the horse's body. When **Angle** these problems occur, the hind end weakens seriously. Raise the heels and extend the shoes way back at the heel. This is effective, but it does not always solve the problem.

These are just representative theories and methods that have worked for me. I have discovered other methods, and developed other

Step By Step ideas for helping horses, but they are being saved for the next, more comprehensive book. The best way to learn Proper Balancing Movement principles is step by step.

Tony Gonzales

Explanations for charts begin on page 208.

P.B.M. Systematic Horse Analysis

1. Normal Balance

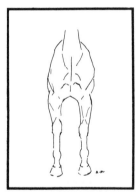

2. Frontal Width Balance

3. Right Shoulder View

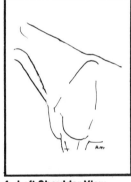

4. Left Shoulder View

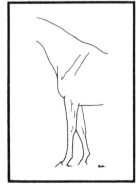

5. Frontal Balance View

Chart 1

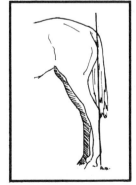

6. Hind Balance View

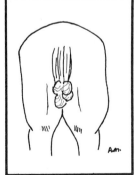

7. Hind Width Balance

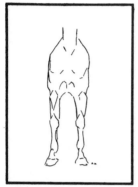

9. Splay Footed

8. Desired Back

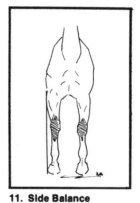

10. Pigeon Toed

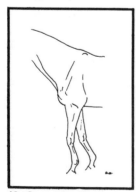

11. Side Balance

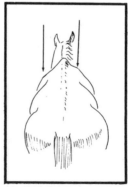

12. Behind the Knee

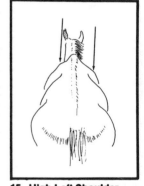

13. Over at the Knee

Chart 2

14. High Right Shoulder

15. High Left Shoulder

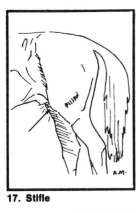

17. Stifle

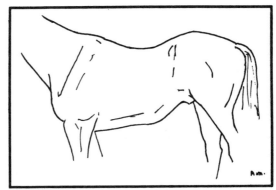

16. Sway Back

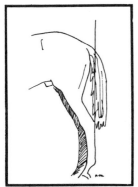

18. Standing Behind

19. Sickle Hock

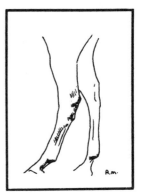

20. Curb

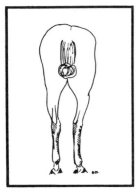

21. High Left Hip

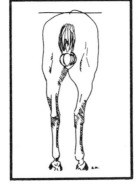

22. High Right Hip

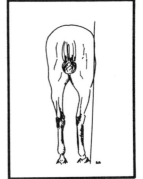

23. Hind Side Balance

Chart 3

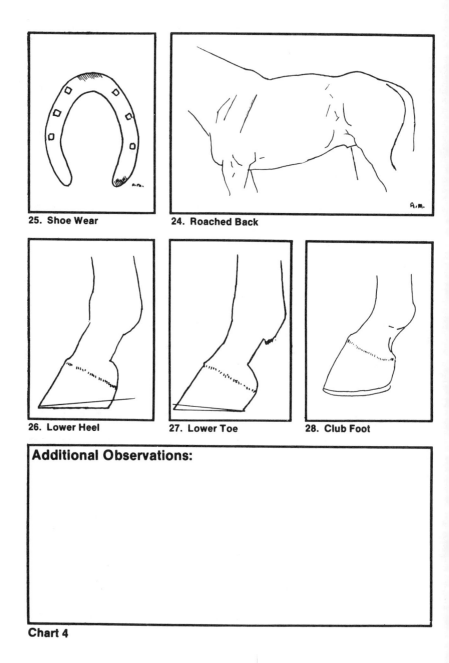

25. Shoe Wear

24. Roached Back

26. Lower Heel

27. Lower Toe

28. Club Foot

Additional Observations:

Chart 4

206

30. Rider Position

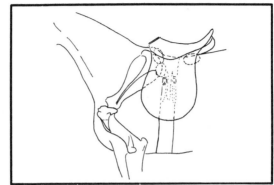

29. Saddle Fit

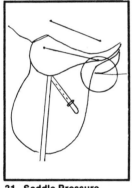

31. Saddle Pressure

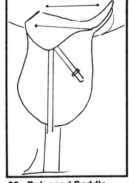

32. Balanced Saddle

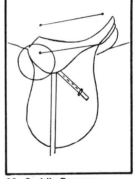

33. Saddle Pressure

Explanation of Charts

These charts are designed to show you where to look at a horse's body in order to understand the philosophy behind P.B.M.

Chart one gives sectional views of the normal parts of a horse's body. The sections will show you where to look for uneven development.

Chart two shows some of the uneven and less desirable conformation faults that horses can have. It shows both the front and the back of a horse. There may, of course, be additional faults, but this is a learner's guide to train your eye.

Chart three represents some of the uneven and less desirable conformation faults of the hind end and back of a horse.

Chart four shows the wear of a shoe, angle adjustment possibilities, and the nature of the foot. This is primarily to help you spot problems caused by lower leg growth.

Chart five demonstrates how uneven a saddle can be on a horse's back, how a rider will sit on an uneven saddle, how the saddle can interfere with the horse's movement, where the saddle pressure is on the horse's back, and how a horse's movement can be affected by a saddle and a rider.

Remember, these charts are only guides. You may run into many things not shown here, but I want you to start training your eye. The possibilities are endless. However, using these guides, you should be able to help explain both lameness and movement problems in a horse. Once you start looking at a horse this way, you will find you can start answering some of your questions for yourself.

The following is a more detailed explanation of each chart. You should learn to approach each horse systematically, so that you have a good understanding of how his whole body works before you try adjusting anything.

Chart one

Picture 1 shows the whole horse, because you should consider the whole horse's conformation when you are looking for inconsistencies in movement and training.

Picture 2 gives a chest view. You should check to see how well developed the chest muscles are and whether the animal is well balanced as to width.

Picture 3 shows the right view of the shoulders. Here you should look at the angle of slope of the shoulders to see if the muscle tone and development are good.

Picture 4 represents the left view of the shoulders. As with picture 3, what you are checking here is slope, muscle development, and which side the mane falls on.

Picture 5 shows the side view of the front legs. This helps determine how balanced a horse is in front, from the neck, chest, legs and hoof, in proportion to the weight carried in the front half of the body.

Picture 6 gives the hind leg position and shows how straight it should be.

Picture 7 is an overall view of the hip, showing how to determine muscle development and even height of the hips.

Chart two

Picture 8 shows the level of a horse's back. This is the preferred look.

Picture 9 represents a narrow chest and splay-footedness (turning out at the toe).

Picture 10 shows a wide check and pigeon toedness (turning in at the toe).

Picture 11 demonstrates how to look for balance of the outer body and the outer wall of the hoof. This is what I call side balance.

Picture 12 shows a horse that is behind at the knee.

Picture 13 depicts a horse that is over at the knee.

Picture 14 is an over the hip view of the shoulders. In this case the horse is higher in the right shoulder and lower in the left.

Picture 15 gives a hip view of the shoulders. In this case the horse is higher in the left shoulder and lower in the right.

Chart three

Picture 16 shows a horse that is sway backed.

Picture 17 represents the stifle area of a horse. You must determine how straight it is.

Picture 18 shows a horse whose legs are behind itself.

Picture 19 depicts a horse that is sickle hocked.

Picture 20 shows a horse that has a curb (calcium on the cannon in the back of the leg below the hock).

Picture 21 is a rear view of the hips. In this case you will note that the hip is rounded, but the left hip is higher than the right.

Picture 22 gives a balance line to check to tell if the hips are level. In this case the right hip is higher and the left hip is lower.

Picture 23 represents side balance of the hind end. This involves lining up the outer muscles of the hips with the outer flare of the hoof wall.

Chart four

Picture 24 shows a horse with a roached back.

Picture 25 depicts shoe wear at the toe or heel.

Picture 26 demonstrates what has to be done to change the angle of the toe, lowering the heel.

Picture 27 shows what has to be done to change the angle of the heel, cutting the toe, and raising the angle.

Picture 28 depicts a club foot.

Chart five

Picture 29 shows how a saddle can interfere with shoulder blade movement.

Picture 30 demonstrates how a rider will sit to compensate for an unbalanced saddle position on a horse's back.

Picture 31 shows the pressure point of a saddle when it is positioned too far back on a horse.

Picture 32 displays a balanced saddle placement.

Picture 33 identifies the pressure point of a saddle when it is too high on the withers.

Bibliography

The Master Farrier $25
President of Oklahoma Farriers College, Bud Beaston covers problems of corrective shoeing and conditions of hoof and leg. Over 250 step-by-step illus. 191 pp.
Source: Bud Beaston, Oklahoma Farriers College, Rt. 2, Box 88, Sperry, OK 74073.

Principles of Horseshoeing II $49.95
Encyclopedia of farrier science and craftsmanship. New and enlarged. Step-by-step instructions on shoemaking and shoeing. Hardbound, 1133 illus., 567 pp.
Source: Doug Butler, P.O. Box 370, Maryville, MO 64468. C.O.D. orders (816) 582-3202.

How To Build Horseshoeing Equipment $10
By Scott Simpson, instructor at University of Montana. Basics of tools and techniques detailed in simple text. Good illus., 100 pp.
Source: Walla Walla Community College, Scott Simpson, Farrier Instr., 500 Tausick Way, Walla Walla, WA 99362.

The Mechanics of Horseshoeing Simplified $10
All the information and illustrations needed to perform an acceptable shoeing job. 60 pp.
Source: Walla Walla Community College, Scott Simpson, Farrier Instr., 500 Tausick Way, Walla Walla, WA 99362.

Mechanics of Shoeing Gaited Horses $10
Gives the basics of this specialization shoeing. Preparation, shaping, fitting, nailing, tricks of the trade and special problems are covered. 118 pp.
Source: Walla Walla Community College, Scott Simpson, Farrier Instr., 500 Tausick Way, Walla Walla, WA 99362.

Because It Works, That's Why

Some have been skeptical. But Proper Balance Movement works to treat lameness and poor performance. It is a concept so simple, so logical, you will wonder why you didn't think of it yourself.

It took the experienced, intuitive eye of Tony Gonzales to see that a horse's movement is influenced as much from the withers down as from the hoof up and that a lasting solution has to address all the angles, from the right shoes to the fit of your saddle.

To learn more about how you and your horse can consistently be your best, visit Tony at one of his clinics or lectures. Read his book *Proper Balance Movement, A Diary of Lameness.* Or arrange with Tony for a private evaluation and see it happen.

For more information, or to schedule a clinic or evaluation, call or write:

Anthony Z. Gonzales
13602 Ellendale Dr.
Chantilly, VA 22021
(703) 378-4763

Proper Balance Movement